THE

QUARTERLY

EDITED BY

GORDON LISH

No few persons have inquired into our practice of not presenting notes on contributors. *The Quarterly* realizes that this practice is at odds with custom among magazine publishers, the notable exception being *The New Yorker.* *The Quarterly*'s position in the matter is this: whatever space would be given over to such news is better given over to what this magazine is about. On this point, *The Quarterly* observes a policy of doing what it can to eliminate notions of the appearance of rank among its contributors, although it certainly happens that the properties of physical objects require one entry to come after another—or before. Finally, this magazine does confess to a bias favoring writers who are emerging over writers who have emerged. To be sure, we have brought out the work of writers who are known widely, and *The Q* will continue to do so as merit warrants. But our aim, which must have been evident from the start but which is now stated openly, bears chiefly on the creating of a venue for writers who will be as new to us as they will be to our readers. *The Quarterly* actively seeks such writers, but admits to only partial success in uncovering them—this for the reason that we cannot know which writers we are looking for until they have let us find them.

THE
QUARTERLY

9/SPRING 1989

VINTAGE BOOKS

A DIVISION OF RANDOM HOUSE

NEW YORK

THE QUARTERLY (ISSN 0893-3103) IS EDITED BY GORDON LISH AND IS PUBLISHED MARCH, JUNE, SEPTEMBER, AND DECEMBER FOR $32 THE YEAR ($45 IN CANADA) BY VINTAGE BOOKS, A DIVISION OF RANDOM HOUSE, INC., 201 EAST 50TH STREET, NEW YORK, NY 10022. APPLICATION TO MAIL AT SECOND-CLASS POSTAGE RATES IS PENDING AT NEW YORK, NY, AND AT ADDITIONAL MAILING OFFICES. SEND ORDERS AND ADDRESS CHANGES TO THE QUARTERLY, VINTAGE BOOKS, SUBSCRIPTION DEPARTMENT, TWENTY-EIGHTH FLOOR, 201 EAST 50TH STREET, NEW YORK, NY 10022. BACK ISSUES MAY BE PURCHASED, BY CHECK OR MONEY ORDER, AT $7.95 THE COPY; ADD $1.50 FOR POSTAGE AND HANDLING OF EACH COPY REQUESTED.

THE QUARTERLY WELCOMES THE OPPORTUNITY TO READ WORK OF EVERY CHARACTER, AND IS ESPECIALLY CONCERNED TO KEEP ITSELF AN OPEN FORUM. MANUSCRIPTS MUST BE ACCOMPANIED BY THE CUSTOMARY RETURN MATERIALS, AND SHOULD BE ADDRESSED TO THE EDITOR, THE QUARTERLY, 201 EAST 50TH STREET, NEW YORK, NY 10022. THE QUARTERLY MAKES THE UTMOST EFFORT TO OFFER ITS RESPONSE TO MANUSCRIPTS NO LATER THAN ONE WEEK SUBSEQUENT TO RECEIPT. OPINIONS EXPRESSED HEREIN ARE NOT NECESSARILY THOSE OF THE EDITOR OR OF THE PUBLISHER.

ISBN: 0-679-72139-8

DESIGN BY ANDREW ROBERTS
MANAGEMENT BY DENISE STEWART AND ELLEN F. TORRON

THIS IS TO ANNOUNCE THAT THE HOB BROUN PRIZE OF 1988 IS PRESENTED TO WILLIAM TESTER, FOR "DARLING," MR. TESTER'S ENTRY IN Q5. SPECIAL MENTION IS MADE OF FOUR OTHER FICTIONS APPEARING IN THE QUARTERLY OVER THE COURSE OF 1988— "THE BOYS ON THEIR BICYCLES," BY HAROLD BRODKEY, "THINKING ABOUT MOMMA," BY JANET MITCHELL, "SWITZERLAND," BY ANN PYNE, AND "FISHBOY," BY MARK RICHARD. THE AWARD OF THE HOB BROUN PRIZE OF 1989 WILL BE ANNOUNCED IN Q13. READERS ARE REMINDED THAT THE HOB BROUN PRIZE IS GIVEN ANNUALLY FOR A WORK OF FICTION, ONE WHOSE REACH IS GREAT AND YET WHOSE EXECUTION SEEMS EFFORTLESSLY IN KEEPING WITH THE AIM, THIS IN THE MANNER OF A BASEBALL PLAYER MUCH ADMIRED BY HOB BROUN. THE HOB BROUN PRIZE WAS ESTABLISHED BY THE QUARTERLY IN 1988 AND IS ADMINISTERED BY THIS MAGAZINE IN COOPERATION WITH MR. AND MRS. HEYWOOD HALE BROUN, IN MEMORY OF THEIR SON.

THE QUARTERLY

9/SPRING 1989

THE QUARTERLY

THE QUARTERLY

THE

QUARTERLY

He confronted
all the men
in turn

The Beauty in Bulls

"Oh, my badness."

"Oh, your badness what?"

"This is a thoroughly bodacious ta-ta business."

"Here, look at this one."

"Oh, and a bodacious walk, bodacious hair, bodacious legs, bodacious badness."

"This is the one where they take him away by horse and cart."

"I bet she's been tupped just now. She has that look of just having been tupped."

"She is not a ewe."

"Hey, why did God create women?"

"There are twenty-six in all—and see, this is the one beforehand, when he is alive and well and in the field."

"I want to come in her hair."

"They say the meat is given to orphans."

"Did you just hear what I said?"

"You want to come in her hair. This is the one where the picadores come out. My God, he almost looks ready for it. Look how he is bending his head low and revealing that neck. That neck of his looks so strong. That neck looks so strong that it looks like there is a man inside of it."

"There is a man inside of my badness."

"Then comes the cape trick."

"Then comes the cape trick."

"Do you remember it?"

"Her ta-tas are the size of teacups."

"There is a roar in the crowd."

"She is a walking hutchful of delicate cups and saucers and bowls."

"Oh, and the blood coming out of his mouth."

"I want to open her glass doors and take down her china."

"You never saw anything so red."

"I want to bring a cup up to my mouth and suck on it so hard that it stays there because of my suck. You know the suck you had when you were a kid? Afterward, I am going to show her the rim it made around my mouth."

"It is a horrible thing to see such a big animal hurt by his own size when he falls on himself. It is just one more thing to happen to him."

"The cup still feels like it is there later, around your mouth."

"Do you think Picasso knew this?"

"Your lips look as if they were in some kind of kissing derby for the last ten days."

"I keep looking at these lines he has drawn. After a while, it looks to me as if the men with their capes could be the bulls, and the bulls rearing, they could be the men. Is that all Picasso, or is that me?"

"Her legs are like candles."

"Jesus, horns."

"I bet you want to ask me which are the tapered ends."

"He has even drawn in the men and the women holding up their white handkerchiefs."

"The ends with the wicks."

"When they could not wave handkerchiefs, they waved anything. They waved cigarette packs."

"Well, I haven't decided yet. Go suck on a candle. A long, thin candle."

"Beer cans."

"Well, it is bodacious."

"Let me count. Six men on foot, three on horseback."

"It is like sucking on her finger."

"Here he has turned around as if to say how dare you. This is the how-dare-you look. This is the how-dare-you-put-that-thing-in-me look. This is the look when the men run behind the little wooden walls. This is when the crowd stands up and cheers for the bull."

"Her eyes are rocks in the water."

"This is when people want to see the bull win because the bull is so strong. This is when people want to see the man die because there is always that possibility and they want to see it happen. They have paid to come in. They want to see it."

"Have you ever pulled the most beautiful rock out of the ocean and put it on your dresser and the next day you look at the rock and you think how you could have ever thought that that rock was beautiful, because now it is so white and dry it is not a rock but a bone?"

"In the end, I would rather take the side of the bull. I would rather see the bull win. He is the stronger of the two. The crowd has paid, but maybe now they forget that that matters, maybe now they are just thinking that they don't even want to look at the man because the man is so weak and they are so embarrassed by the man."

"I will never suck her eyes out."

"They all want to be bulls now."

"I will never suck her beautiful eyes out."

"The crowd, all of them in the crowd, want to be bulls."

"To have them go white on my dresser top."

"And when the man wins, when the bull is stuck, they are so relieved. They never did want to be bulls. Who knows what a bull does, anyway? they say. Let the man win, they say. Up go the handkerchiefs."

"Can you hear it when he's stuck?"

"It is like sticking a knife into meat and pulling it out. It *is* sticking a knife into meat and pulling it out. It goes *thwack*."

"*Thwack?*"

"If they are good, then the ears go; if they are really good, then also goes the tail."

"I have tried to put those rocks back into tap water. But it does no good."

"The women want the ears. The women want the tails. Whatever do they do with them? It is enough to imagine that all the beautiful women could possibly be living in houses with trunkfuls of bull ears and bull tails. Because only the beautiful women are given the ears and the tails."

"Maybe it is why God created beautiful women."

"This is my favorite one. See how the man is down on one knee in front of the bull and the cape, too, is down on the ground? This shows the bull is ready, this shows the bull could if he wanted to."

"Maybe I am confusing things here, maybe she has never ever been tupped before. Maybe this is what my bodacious badness is picking up."

"She is not a ewe."

"I want to be her first."

"I respect the banderilleros."

"There would be a world opened unto her."

"In this one, they sit in a chair and wait for the bull. The bull's tail is saying, *What are you doing? Don't you know?*"

"She will remember me for the rest of her life. And it is not an only-girl thing, it is anyone's thing. I remember my first. Everyone remembers their first. Really everyone's first is not unmemorable. Or maybe I mean everyone's first is barely memorable, because what is bigger in all world at that moment is that you are doing it. Here is where it all falls apart. Here is where I really wonder do I want to be her first."

"*Salto con la garrocha,* jump with the javelin."

"But how will I know I will be her first unless I am her first? There is no way to tell. Over dinner, over coffee."

"*Echar perros al toro,* thrown to the dogs."

"But she will tell me just before I am about to begin to suck on her cups."

"Picasso is my hero."

"If I am her first or eighty-first."

"Oh, eighty-one, that's a lot."

"For anyone's ta-tas."

"When you get to number forty, you are already in the bodacious zone."

"Yes, I know the bodacious zone."

"Shh, I am thinking."

"This bull's thing is big. This thing is monstrous. This bull makes me feel stumpy. Outdone by a bull. Next thing you know, she will be wanting this bull."

"I remember being there and wanting a drink because of the sight of the blood. But then I became used to it and I watched, and at the end, when they dragged the bull around and he became dirty on his back, I liked it."

"If your first is a bull, then are you part bull the rest of your life? Does it make her, then, a cow? I cannot believe she stooped to do it with a bull. Oh, she is some cow."

"How many bulls a day?"

"Will that bull suck on her cups?"

"Imagine, all the orphans. Oh no, not bull again! they say at the table."

"When he is done with her, that bull, he will take her eyes out with his horns."

"Bull soup."

"Let me at that bull."

"My aunt has been invited to a dinner, and Rey Juan Carlos will be there."

"Oh?"

"My aunt can't believe they are serving quenelles cooked in Madeira and amontillado."

"That bodacious Rey Juan Carlos."

"Oh, to see their faces if bull soup was served."

"Damn, that bull's thing is big."

"Do you really think he walks around that ring thinking, *My God, look, everyone, look how really big my thing is?*"

"No."

"He is thinking, *Why am I here, what can I do?*"

"Why am I here and what can I do?"

"That's right. That is the whole nine yards."

"Tell your aunt to say so at the dinner, then."

"I would have loved to have been a fly on the wall when Picasso was drawing these things."

"How big was Picasso's thing?"

"Did they come to him in a dream?"

"Artists all have small things."

"Say *bull tongue* over and over again and see what does it sound like."

"I am no artist."

"Botha, Botha, Mr. South Africa."

"Why am I here? What can I do? I have a thing so big."

"Bull is a specialty over there in South Africa."

"I will drown her."

"Bodacious Botha."

"Imagine wanting to do it with a bull. How does she do it? Does she swallow?"

"If you are to be her first, then what will she know from swallowing?"

"She has swallowed it from the bull."

"There is beauty in bulls."

"And not in cows?"

"Picasso did not draw cows."

"He should have. Let me tell you about cows. Cows are big. It is insane to think that they could never hurt you. But they do not. It makes you think, Is the cow so big to size up with the bull? And only with the bull?"

"Let me look at that girl."

"Now we both have our bodacious badness on."

"When you get to her, you will not have to think, *Why am I here and what can I do?*"

"No, I will say, 'Look at me. See the size my thing is. I will do what I must do.' " **Q**

Gumby Goes for a Drive

Gumby comes out of a bar riding this guy's hip like a baby learning the Australian crawl. Gumby, a life-sized plastic doll, is a foot shorter than the guy carrying him, is Play-Doh green, and inflated, but is slowly losing air. If Gumby talked, with his yellow triangle smile, you'd expect a chirp.

The guy has just stepped out of the Giant Palm. The new air feels like a damp washcloth. He is on the edge of the curb, rocking, in fresh running shoes, on the balls of his feet and waiting for an oil truck to get down the hill and out of his way. In the trailing diesel cloud, his Kool turns bitter, so he tosses it away. Then he reaches over his shoulder to pull at the collar of his tennis shirt and bends Gumby's back. His leather jacket squeaks, as if there were tiny mice inside.

With the truck gone, he steps across the yellow line. When he gets to their brown, rebuilt Toyota Celica, he sees that the meter has expired. He plants his right foot on an encyclopedia-sized mud spot above the rear wheel well, digs an elbow into Gumby's back, and tugs at the door. The guy's wife, in a black leather dress and too-big glasses with red plastic frames, stares straight ahead, finishing a Marlboro.

Her husband says, "Aahharr," until the door opens. She looks over, and as her cigarette hand moves to her forehead, the silver chains on her wrist click.

"Thought I was going to rot," she says, punching EJECT. A Monkees cassette pops out.

Gumby goes into the back, his pointed head catching on the rear window defroster's aluminum ridges. "Come on," her husband says. "Gumby goes for a drive."

Gumby won't fit.

The guy reaches down to unleash the bucket seat. It springs forward with a quick thump. The guy drags Gumby's square legs inside and folds him in two. Gumby's face slides around until it is pressed, still smiling, into the triangular window behind the woman's right ear. He seems ready to peek over her shoulder. One green leg flops down between the seats, brushing the parking-brake handle.

"You know," the woman says, feeling around for matches under the maps and bank receipts in the dusty front of the dash, "I bet boxers make better fathers." She lights the new cigarette and snaps her wrist, shaking out the match.

When the guy left, they were arguing about why they only vacuum once the cat starts throwing up. This new question bothers him. He is neither a boxer nor a father. "Better than what," he says, "German shepherds?"

She blows smoke against the tinted sunroof. "Better than airline pilots, I bet. They've got discipline. What's an airline pilot going to teach a kid? How to pack?"

"Scheduling, efficiency, vision. How's that?" The keys clink like change as he takes them from his pocket. He starts the car. It idles fast, and he turns and says, "High, stable incomes. That they have."

"I mean if a kid's father is a boxer, a Lou, a Bonebuster, that kid's got something."

"Like what?" the guy says. "Like brain death? You get what you get."

The guy swats Gumby's leg and releases the parking brake. As he takes his hand away, the green leg swings back, nestling against his thigh. He cranks the wheel, glances over his shoulder, and hits the gas once. The Celica lurches halfway out of the space. The woman leans across to look out her husband's window, resting her cigarette hand on Gumby's leg.

Two kids on skateboards scream down the hill behind the Celica. Both are wearing surfing shirts, Jam's, and purple high-tops with Day-Glo laces. To these two kids, their soft plastic wheels sound like distant jets. The first, sitting, in the fatigue jacket, shouts, "We be thrashing."

The guy hits the gas and the Celica jumps.

The woman says "Yeow" when she spots the tall blond kid in the sliver of rear window above Gumby's side. The kid is standing, knees bent, hands out like tiny wings. The guy sees him in the mirror, lifts off the gas, and clamps the brakes as the kid he didn't see rolls past his front left tire.

The woman's cigarette touches Gumby's leg. They watch the skateboards snake through the intersection as the smell of melting vinyl rises slowly between them.

"Stupid kids," she says.

Chirp. **Q**

SHEILA KOHLER

In Amber

Here she lies, looking as though she were asleep—
does she not?—lying under the gauze of the mosquito net, in
the strange light of this shuttered room. Would you care to sit
awhile by her side? You are the first to arrive and, as such, sir,
will be my special guest. This iron bed where she lies, with the
bars at the head and at the feet, is a bed that belonged to my
great-grandmother, you know; it is also the bed where I was
born. Now my wife lies here, unmoving, a picture of innocence
and peace—not so? Notice how the faint lamplight glimmers
on her white neck, lights up her wavy hair, and catches the lilt
of a thigh. A beautiful woman—is she not?—as beautiful as a
Botticelli.

Perhaps you are right, more beautiful than a Botticelli.

Let me draw the curtains over the windows to keep the
room cool and dark. I have always liked the rooms of this
house kept dark, with the shutters tightly closed against the
sun and the air and the view of these flat fields. I carry this land
in my head; I have no need to look. I know each branch, each
footpath, each blade of grass. This place has been ours, of
course, for as long as the white man has been here.

I was always telling her that closed shutters keep a room
cool, that dust and sunlight suck the colors from fabrics, warp
the furniture, and that open windows are just an invitation for
flies. And flies, of course, bring disease. One has to be particularly careful with flies in a place like this, does one not? One
never knows where the flies might have been: the suppurating
eyes, the open wounds, the compost heap. But she insisted on
fresh air, on sunlight. She would walk around this room half-
naked, with the curtains open, visible to any native or pass-
erby. As for the flies, she maintained flies never came near her.
She said she had no need for this mosquito net. Insects, she

insisted, feared her. She often boasted that she was never ill; never caught cold or ran a fever. It is true that she had a remarkable appetite, did she not? I would watch her eat, fascinated. She liked eggs, fish, meat—huge quantities of meat, it seemed to me, eating it half-raw, picking the bones. Once, I found her lying like this in this bed, propped up on those big, white, lacy pillows, her hair loose about her, picking on a lamb bone. And the fruit she could consume! I can see her biting into a guava, taking the top off the fruit with those teeth and then tipping back her head and squeezing the juice and pips into her mouth, the orange liquid trickling down her chin onto those heavy breasts.

It never ceased to amaze me, for someone who seemed— how shall I put it?—so full of life—how heavily she slept. She could sleep, it seems to me, endlessly. When I came off the land at noon, I would still find her here, in this bed, dreaming. She would rise then and bathe, join me on the veranda, half-dressed, her thick hair rapidly braided and hanging like a damp loose rope down her back. She would drink a beer or two, to whet her appetite, she would say. By the time I left to go back to my work, she would be asleep again, sweating in the heat, her hair clinging to her brow. At night, sometimes, unable to sleep, I would watch her breast rising and falling. Ah, such a young and healthy woman, was she not? Whoever would have thought it could come to this? According to the report, she died of something that drained away her strength, gradually, leaving her with nothing but that strong lithe body you see here, and the beautiful face.

In this heat it will not last long.

I have always liked the heat, even on the worst of days, when the sun beats down mercilessly on this corrugated-iron roof. Perhaps my ancestors came, originally, from some hot country similar to this, and perhaps hers, despite her dark coloring, came from the North. She would sit here on hot days like this, turning pink in the face, fanning herself with that heart-shaped straw fan you see on the dresser top (I've left everything exactly the way she liked it), gasping for air. How can anyone live in such a climate, she would say. I'm afraid she found this place very boring, you see. Wildlife was of no interest to her, as you must know, and she had no time, she said, for flowers or for trees. What she liked, she would tell me constantly, were people. She liked talking to almost anyone. She would strike up a conversation with a perfect stranger. In the evenings, when I came back into the house, I often found her lounging at the kitchen table, chatting to the cook. When she wanted to, she could talk very well. When she was in the. mood, there was no one more charming, was there now? No one I knew seemed able to resist her. You know, she was doing me a favor in letting me serve her, and it would have been impolite to decline.

I was never impolite, I assure you.

It was she who persuaded our neighbor to sell me that field. I never did understand why she wanted all those clothes she never wore. She was a generous woman, very generous; the sight of poverty always brought tears to her eyes—she hated, particularly, to see a native suffer. She gave lavish gifts.

Of course, in the end, it was I who paid.

Yes, I am used to the silence here, but it seems to me the silence is slightly changed. It is a different silence now. Things will not be quite the same. Perhaps you find it strange that I can sit here by her side. She always said that she found me tiresome because I never spoke of what I felt, but now look. She complained that we never went anywhere, but I must manage this estate, you know, and spend my evenings with my books. An ornithologist friend of mine would come to dine with us once a week. I had intended to move on, you know, but where, sir, would I find a house with such thick walls, such tall trees that cast such deep shade: those eucalyptus, their sickle-shaped leaves shimmering silver in the sun, were planted by my ancestors all around this property, you see; where could I find a place where I could rise at dawn and step into such light, such space, the horizon so distant?

Oh, I knew she was not happy. But no one is happy.

The breasts, if you look at the breasts carefully, you may actually find, as I do, that they are rather too large.

I was so very nice to her. Sir, I was always so nice to her. I took certain measures. I took every measure.

Still, all this is very surprising to me. Nevertheless, there is no denying it—there is the report, and her face.

Must you leave so soon? Before you go, do be a good fellow and taste her plum cake. Q

The Fucking Jerk I Used to Fuck

All this I told the nun, her nodding and watching from a distance, me sobbing and hiccupping like a fool in her emergency room, hating her for looking as though a nun could know anything about anything, and saying over and over—so she won't start thinking she's got something on me—how I don't believe in God or any of that stuff—even though I can't help liking her sweet-old goddamn nun-twinkly eyes—the stiff white around the face and neck and the flowing black everywhere else—the way she might appear in a dream about nuns gliding birdlike through a cemetery on top of a cliff above the water—the water rough and hard to cross, and the cliff high with rocks that leave their marks on you—and I can't help pouring it out to her about the man whose voice we hear from up the hall, strapped down now and still screaming, "She's the Devil! She's the Devil!" so the whole hospital can hear and come around to see what kind of loonies have swooped in this time—the way the pale, faraway doctors and nurses and orderlies stood around staring when the two of us roared and cartwheeled in here like bad-tripping harpies, me looking for a shot of something for him to come down on, him looking for I never did figure out what.

All this I shouted to that blue-eyed doctor as they pulled that careening bull-heavy body onto a cart and started strapping the big arms that could have broken me in two if I hadn't gotten him down here after the acid went bad on us—him bawling, "Heart attack!" falling on the floor, then jumping up, running through the house, up and down the stairs, rolling his eyes at the ceiling, ducking his head, yelling he'd be trapped in there forever—and me chasing after with "It's me! It's me!" and him looking like my face was snakes, and me thinking, Could it really be his heart?

So he's still looking that way, ropy veins raised along the sides of his head, and the doctor and the orderlies push him, still heaving, back and forth on that cart with a wheel stuck-wobbling like a grocery cart down the fluorescent hallway, past a starched nurse standing, gaping—a fish looking out of a fish tank. And also past the nun padding up like a long-ago-high-school-play-nun costume I used to have, and she gives me an eye that is not as if I am from outer space, so I go along with her, after I let the still-gaping nurse know that she should get lost now. And all of this I'm crying as we're walking, the nun's black robe swaying over her soft feet like the nuns we spied on as children, when I saw myself galloping in, banshee with torch, pillaging their tombstones, pulling up their lawn. She doesn't say anything back to *Don't you see it's this God stuff that's his problem?* but just watches me, her eyes bland, the tiny spider-veins purpling the contours of her face like markings on a pale lizard. So I go ahead with how we laughed all the time, jumping on beds like children, going dancing with the queers downtown—all this until all the pictures and letters from all those Born Againers up in Tulsa begging him to give up the Life of Sin and return to the Bosom of Jesus got him to thinking God wanted him to go back to his wife. After that, I'm saying—and the old nun doesn't react—it's more than just a little weed, and then he's up there at some resort giving God a chance to have his way with—Shazam!—making him a hard-on for his wife, and I'm down here borrowing money from my sister to buy Christian Dior nightgowns at Neiman's, and getting her to agree with *Why can't he see that our love is holy?* But he doesn't stop for a minute from running back and forth between me and her, the fucking getting rougher and rougher, and him always wanting me to kneel down beside the bed and pray to God with him to make it be as good with her as it is with me. All this time, the nun and I are hearing the yelling and scream-ing from up the hall, and I'm saying, *Why don't they give him a shot?* And she turns these pallid, nearly white eyes back on me, saying nothing as I am pleading that I had to bring him down because I couldn't handle him, and now he'll be mad at me for it after all the misery we had, with him twisting and turning in his seat and nearly jumping from the car a few times—me tripping also and driving with my hand wound up to the wrist into his shirt, scared of the new freeways but going slow out Mockingbird, the lights streaming by, giant writhing glow-worms warbling, *Come this way, this way*—but I'm studying close on the road as we go, so we don't drive on and on, ghostriders on this highway-in-the-sky, endlessly wandering in this woeful Oldsmobile, me crying and hiccupping, and him rocking and moaning, "Oh, God, help me. Oh, Jesus, save me. Please, Jesus, God, and Mary, lend me your hand—I can't get through it alone. Oh, God, when are you going to come, when are you ever going to come and save me—oh, God, please—from all of this?" **Q**

The Backswing of the Slugger

Baseball has always been everything, but baseball isn't the question anymore. I've become a fractional human being all by my own doing, and now, goddamnit, that fraction's been snuffed out, too.

At the end of August the manager of the St. Louis farm team in Orthrup, New York, called me into his office. I wasn't too surprised to be going to the majors—it had taken longer than I'd expected. I figured I'd have to say goodbye to my new girlfriend, if I could get hold of her. I didn't care either way. The manager, Tim Bixy—a name like that, can you believe it? —said I wasn't good enough to play pro ball and I should go home. It was like being told I was dead by the funeral director while no one else was watching. There wasn't even someone to look at for consolation.

I have a lot of trouble liking myself, and I don't doubt that you will, too. I'm a mean and cynical person, and that's rough when you're young. It makes you look shallow. People say all kinds of sincere bullshit, like "I'm trying to find myself." I envy them a little, because they're honest to themselves. But I say, "Yeah, well, why don't you look under your hat for starters."

I would never let anyone else do what I've done to myself.

Last Friday, I tried fucking my new girlfriend up her asshole. I was past the point of asking. I just pulled my prick out of her cunt and tried. I tried for damn near an hour. She was in tears. Grinding my teeth and practically making my hair fall out, sweat pouring into my eyes. A last angry rush. I gave up and we lay side by side. We rested. She begged me not to try again.

My new girlfriend is very new. It's August and I've been in Orthrup since late June. I'm honestly surprised it's lasted this long, but maybe that's because she didn't know me very well. Or because she doesn't have much else to look forward to in Orthrup. My old girlfriend was different.

My family got rich from baseball because my father is a good listener. He didn't pay any attention until he came to see me play once. I played first base that year, because I was the tallest kid. Tall and thin, not much of a wing. That developed later. My mother (she came to watch every week) said to him, "Look at the mess he's made around first base with his spikes. He's so excited."

Between every pitch, I did a little trip around the base, the path, the edge of the grass, picked up pebbles, ripped uneven clumps out by their roots, smoothed the packed dirt with my spikes, rocked back and forth, heel-toe, heel-toe, until the pitcher started up again. If ever I loved someone, it was baseball. I loved the *things* about it. The moments when nothing seemed to be happening. The feeling of the fine dust settling in my nostrils was as important to me as the base runners. That's what I miss the most, the baseballness of baseball, and I realize that as the years went on, I let it slip away and didn't notice.

I hit a home run that game, like almost every game. I had a strong swing. I drove with my hips, shoulders, lips, my unmoving eyes, determinedly into the ball, the sweet spot on the bat. I've always had pop in my bat.

You can't see the ball at all the last seven feet to the plate. Legions of Little League managers say, "Watch the ball hit your bat," but you can't possibly do it. You can distract yourself trying. I've never seen a home run jump off my bat, but I've felt them in my hands, on the sweet spot on the bat.

My father heard me hit. And since we lost that day, he also heard the furious silence on my face. He must have thought, Why does this game make so much noise? His feet, his hands, his face.

Imagine a famous political columnist in the dugout of the New York Yankees on a colorless spring day, asking questions like a jerk. My father. This man who once asked the President, "Why do you love children?" and who produced that famous answer, three columns long. Who once asked another question, "What would you say to Karl Marx if you met him today?" In short, a stupid man who asked stupid questions. But I give him credit, because baseball is a game of stupid questions. Question: "Why does Stottlemeyer wear a long-sleeved sweatshirt even in this heat?" Answer: "To keep his arm warm." And they say good managers are geniuses. Earl Weaver, a famous genius, said, "I play him every day because he's good."

I hate my old girlfriend. I have always hated my old girlfriends. You know what I said to my new girlfriend? I told her my old girlfriend never wanted to suck my cock. I said she always asked me to eat her out, but she never liked to suck my cock.

I hate my sister because she never fucked me.

My father took us to Ft. Lauderdale every spring from '71 to '75. I had a catch with Willie Mays one morning. Just until his arm came around. I played catch with ballplayers' kids, other sportswriters' kids, just kids like me. My father was a sportswriter then, even though he despised the title. He still wanted to be called a journalist. My mother and sister sometimes met us for lunch. Who knows or cares what else they did.

I had a great time as a kid. I was a fucking fool. The old men who watched the game said I had enthusiasm, and they were right. I got up in the morning and I played baseball and watched baseball, and sometimes I had lunch with my parents, usually when my mother had had a shit fit the night before and said baseball was breaking up the family. My stupid sister sat there during those tirades, seriously nodding. But I figured she didn't care any more than I did. She was just taking sides.

For a while I took the trouble to wonder why my sister was never on my side anymore, but then I gave up. After lunch, I played baseball.

In the old neighborhood, before my father used to take us to Ft. Lauderdale every spring, I played baseball on our Little League team, called the Kings, because the King Apartment Buildings were our sponsor. It was lucky, because there were kids that played for a funeral home and a kosher butcher, and I say, Who could take himself seriously with a name like one of those on your uniform?

I used to get the bus out to the field early. I mean, early like before the first worm could even be coaxed out of bed by the very earliest bird. I would get the bus that was still standing in the terminal from the night before, and wait for the driver and the dispatcher to come in from the coffee shop. I'd sit way in the back and put my glove on the seat next to me so that no one would sit there. There wasn't much chance of that, because I was usually the only passenger for the first half of the run. As we got closer to the shopping center in Jackson Heights, the bus started to fill up with old ladies, and then after we passed it, the bus got nearly empty again.

One time, an oval-headed old man in a loose, dark suit climbed on at the terminal. I had him pegged right off as a scout for the Giants or Braves. When he got off two stops before the end, I was disappointed, but I hardly missed my stride. I figured he needed a cup of coffee. Fuck him. Fuck scouts.

The field was wedged up against the bay between La-Guardia and Butler Aviation Field, on a rocky bunch of acres owned by the city. Out on the bay was Rikers Island, a prison. I always dreamed of hitting a ball out there, an impossibility, and beaning a con with it. Alone, of course, I chucked rocks up in the air and caught them in my trusty glove. I practiced my swing with a short stick I found by the water. It was an hour before Vinnie ever showed up, and then some other guys with a real ball. I had forgotten all about the scout back then.

That's the kind of thing I've lost track of. These days, all I think about is the scouts.

Shit.

I'd been lying in bed with my new girlfriend all week-end, though at her insistence as far apart in a twin bed as physically possible. Friday, I'd tried to fuck her up the ass again and we hadn't been outside since. We had pizza and soda delivered four times, and I made her answer the door. I wasn't getting out of bed for anything, and my girlfriend looks like a real slut. Especially in her bare feet, in one of my T-shirts that's too big for her. Let the asshole get a look at what I can still have, I was thinking, of course.

Rusty Staub had just been traded to the Tigers, and my father was sitting with him in the dugout. I don't know how I could stand it, because my father was so stupid. For some kids, it's a treat to watch their fathers at work, but not for me. He asked questions with his hands folded like a napkin on his notepad and stared at Staub. I could see Staub laughing inside.

My old girlfriend had nothing to do with baseball. She was there, but she didn't have anything to do with it. She was there, though, a blurry bridge between two parts of my life.

"It's too hot outside," I said to my new girlfriend. I wanted to tell her more about my old girlfriend. I wanted to stifle my old girlfriend to death with the thick yarn of my voice.

My old girlfriend left me my junior year. She was a cheer-leader, and she left me for a quarterback.

Can you beat it?

I hate her so much I can't remember ever having liked her.

It might be easy to blame my father. He stepped in and spoiled the game for me. He took the fun out. But it's always too easy to blame fathers. Besides, he's too stupid to have had an impact.

My arm was as strong as ever, and I was playing short-stop. I was deep in the hole, grinding my teeth and hoping the guy was going to hit it to me so I could gun him down and end the game.

Frank was pitching, and he deserved to get the win. He wasn't the greatest pitcher I ever saw, and he didn't even have his usual stuff that day, but we needed him to come through and he was pulling it off. He was fighting like hell.

We gave him a big cushion early, mostly because of a three-run homer I hit in the first. After three, we were up 7–2, and it looked like a laugher. But their third pitcher was setting us down, and their shortstop was having a great game. His name was Chuckie Burek, and his father, Chuckie Sr., was the manager. Chuckie Burek was an asshole who'd as easily punch your teeth out with the ball as tag you on the hip. I hated him, the other top shortstop in the league.

Every inning, Frank got into trouble, and then got out of it, but not without giving up a run. But anyway, it was the last inning and we were only up by two, and they had two runners in scoring position.

Vinnie and I visited Frank on the mound. The catcher's always got to know what's going on. It's in their nature. I was there because I felt it was important for me to put in an appear-ance. The three of us stood there. It was three guys on a little hill, no wind, nothing to say. Everyone is allowed their little drama. There were no words exchanged finally. I patted Frank on the rump with my glove, winked at Vinnie, the only other kid from the neighborhood gang to make the team, and then we went back to our positions.

Frank was alone on the mound again, the ball tucked away from the batter. He was concentrating on the target and breathing heavily. He had a huge round chest to draw power from, and a long pitcher's face.

The ball should have been past me. But I was too fast, too good that day. Almost on the outfield grass, I planted my foot and threw to first.

The ball sang; one moment it hovered in place, the next it was in Thatcher's glove at first.

Like in a cartoon.

The game was over on an outstanding play by me. I had won the game with my bat and my hands and my arm.

My new girlfriend asked me what happened. Since I'd known her, she hadn't asked me any questions, and even better, she didn't expect me to talk.

A week before the major-league draft, I took a walk with my sister, who was my only friend. I loved her to the roots of my hair and I couldn't forgive her for hating me. I tried to hold her hand, but she jerked it away. She stared straight ahead.

"You're such a dick," she said. "I can't believe it, but you're worse than Dad. I used to have hope for you. You used to be a human being even though you were a shitty brother. All you care about is baseball, baseball, baseball. And yourself. You tore yourself apart from everything, from your family, from Tom, from Crane."

Who the hell was Crane?

I was claimed by the Cardinals in the twenty-first round of the June Amateur Draft. It was the wrong round, the wrong league, and a standard contract. But I signed it anyhow.

"A very small percentage of kids get picked at all. You should be proud," my father said.

He was right. But even he knew it wasn't good enough.

I took a dinky apartment in Orthrup, which is where the Cardinal farm team plays in the New York Penn League. It's the lowest of the low, but I figured they'd recognize their mistake and call me up to St. Louis soon. I figured I'd demand a trade at the end of the season.

      I chased my new girlfriend around with a baseball bat. I yelled and slipped on a pizza box and made so much noise in general that someone called her brother and he came around with three friends. She told him everything was all right, go away. I sat in one corner of the room, holding the bat, and she sat in the opposite corner, watching me and catching her breath. She didn't have the brains or something to get a knife. She didn't know it, but for a minute I would have let her do it to me.

      So where does a guy go when he's lost everything?

      I don't mean this to sound like despair, but I better get some answers soon. **Q**

Higher Education

They traveled without maps on a perpetual journey, Horlick and Horticulteur and their dog, Sleep. The slutty mother, the child who got so old, and the yellow-eyed dog that sat way in the back, cruising under its own fur, suffering under its own weight, devouring the car, making the inside of the roof hang down like Spanish moss, taking off the door handles one by one, removing the stuffing from the seats, turning the automobile into Sweet Water Bend, yawning and showing fangy teeth and wet gray gums, breathing doggily, emitting a noise, producing the sound of a car-eating dog.

In the beginning there was birth and death.

There was no copulation.

All the birds were in one bush. No eggs were in the basket.

For Horlick there had been the long haul through the canal, which resembled the Panama Canal but which was really the Nepal Canal or the Monkey Canal. No matter, it was one and the same to Horlick.

Dark, lonely, long, sandy. Horlick on the canal. The lazy drift or the violent sloshing.

Ah, birth.

Some years later, one of the Miami cousins confided that ordinarily, when she met a man, she would say, "Don't let this make you nervous, but I am a serious person."

Then, as it happened, the men in the cousin's life stepped quietly back into the words of their own lives. "But still," the cousin whispered, "still, there are the river trips, the river men." There was, for example, the oil rigger from the Ukraine whose tent the cousin shared on the Thames.

On every journey, the cousin explained to those who knew nothing of rivers, on every journey there is one lucky twosome, one woosome twosome, who, well, let us state it this way: The other river-trekkers are getting sand out of their shoes and eating wet pie and taking pictures of rock formations and wondering why the toilet paper does not seem to be made of toilet paper and exchanging wet telephone numbers, while there is the woosome twosome, who have somehow vanished, slipped away, who lie, even now, far above the winding river, in the warm lap of fallen pines, beneath the hot-mouthed sun, turning passionately in the vaporous vapors.

"What can I say?" the cousin cried. "Am I forever to be despised for my not being one of the ones eating wet pie?"

At Horlick's birth, there was not much there. A pool of something glue-colored, wax-colored, soft. Already vaguely edible, succulent. That was Horlick.

Already wheezing, frantic for companionship, and the parents not there, the mother already slipping into the rubber bathing shoes, preparing for a geological tour of the Lake Superior shoreline. By the end of the first week, when Horlick was developing the defeated stance of the professional snorkeler, this mother was below the bluffs of the Ojibwa Indian Reservation, hip deep in the icy water, bending way over and retrieving locally famous Ice Age concretions. The odd smooth stones that looked like baby heads, or what the mother referred to as the male member. Horlick's father was not there, either. He was out at the racetrack—flutter flutter of the flags and his ice-cream shoes beneath the peanut-colored hat and his love-of-life eyebrows—shrieking, "Go, Prairie Chicken, go!" Screaming, "Hey, Baby Frank Lloyd, do it!"

It was a time of war.

Fires were being lit.

Tinfoil was being wadded.

Balls were weighed in at small city parks. Women in nurse's uniforms sat at card tables and asked that people knit washcloths and send them overseas.

You know where that is? Overseas?

It was suggested that Horlick be sent to a brewery for fattening up. Or to a turkey farm, where the birds would gather in warming huddles and offer her a sense of feathered love. The family, so busy planting victory gardens, hilariously harvesting Horlick's popcorn and watermelon beds, manufacturing bombs for Our Boys, closed their eyes and lifted their trumpets in a single blast, one—two—three, all together now: It's a long way to Tip—per—ary, it's—a—long—way—to—go . . .

Horticulteur. Gift of brief love. Direct from Horlick's hothouse. Fatherless, because as Horlick would sometimes point out, the love affair, the first leg of what might be called life's journey *together,* had not taken. During the wedding ceremony, Horticulteur's father had set first himself and then the chapel on fire. Lighting a cigar out of habit and a general vagueness as to what was going on around him, the groom soon discovered the cuff of his trousers to be smoldering, discovered the hair on his leg to be singeing, discovered the need for a helping hand, but as it happened, Old Father Hairshirt was otherwise occupied. As it happened, the bridal couple—the groom-father in his white tie and tails and the bride in her pink-and-blue taffeta, the yards of illusion veil, the bouquet of baby's breath and gardenias and dogwood and tulips and lilacs and brave zinnias and bachelor buttons and avocados and old ratty palm fronds trembling over the faint bulge that was Horticulteur—were left twiddling their ring fingers and giving birth to disaster, because Silence Please I Am Speaking Directly to God had buried his Episcopalian robes and his pearly chin in the gold chalice behind the altar, and by the time something wet was required to quash the flames, the cup was empty.

Oh, the bare backside, people said as the years passed. Oh, the flapping tails. Oh, the firelight and the owls hooting in the treetops and the snow falling and falling on the churchyard and on the ice walls along the Lake Michigan shore, on the flatlands where it drifted against the sagging snow fences, on the birch trees and the lonely pines at Lac du Flambeau, on the towns along the Mississippi, on Red Wing and Pepin and

Moose Junction, and on the moonlit backside of the bare
broom of the groom, as the father of someone whose dear
sweet heartbeat was then no more than a sigh flew through the
altar door and out across the snow-covered fields.

Horlick refused to elaborate.

Said only, To endure you need seams.

That time she left home for good.

Horticulteur. A vision in pink angora, in calm sponge-
colored stadium boots, in every climate, in any weather, baked
to her bovine pink pads, so unstintingly hungry, so voluptuous
in her overwhelming pastel expanse, like a suburban garden,
like a patch of rhododendron and snapdragon and gladiola
and tiny benches and little bridges and stone people peeking
out, like the horizon itself come to fly behind them, riding
along with them into the interminable adult years. Horlick,
looking out one twilit evening at something rising above the
side window, saw that it was Horticulteur on the running
board, flung up like a ship's head.

Crazy about each other from the beginning, the mother
and daughter stopped talking for a time after the college
debacle.

You could have done it for me, Horlick had cried after Horticulteur had refused to send the application in to Yale. *My only
child. This one thing. For the poor mother. Who would have had something to talk about at cocktail parties in any city for the rest of her life!*

Horticulteur had protested: You knew I didn't drive. I had
no outfits. I didn't add.

On they went. The slutty mother, the men who said,
"We'll meet again, without a shadow of a doubt," the child
who got so old, and the yellow-eyed dog that cruised along
under thinning fur.

The landscape changed but appeared unchanged. There

was little California, with sports cars flying off of cliffs into the starry nights, a man eating Christmas-tree lights by the side of the road, things, things. Then Connecticut, where the hors d'oeuvres were smaller and the leaves a deadly shade of black-green. Where the Southern woman they liked so much sat on a bench waiting for an afternoon wedding to begin, watching the cake lean into the summer sun, smiling and drinking her bourbon, looking toward the hills, saying to her son, who had come to see what his mother was up to, "Ah em just sitten heah," looking over the rim of her glass toward the hills and Jesus.

On a Friday during a year of unrest, the threesome found themselves deep in the countryside of a new land and spotted the Southern woman again, and waved and waved. So glad to see an old friend in a foreign backwater!

Sleep, honey, give your hallelujah chorus.

Hey, there, Memphis Mommy, what you all up to? Horlick shouted.

How *you* all?

Memphis Mommy, you want to come with us? You remember Sleep?

How you is, Sleep?

Share your bourbon with old friends?

Do a deer.

Re a ray.

What you think of these ratty old palms, Memphis Mommy called. Little old natives. Little old people burning heads on sticks. Uman eads? Screaming way to hell and gone?

You come on with us, Mommy. Sleep can move on over.

Screaming to all git-out. And those little old mosquitoes all puffed up with malaria?

Mommy, you lookin' old as sin and peelin' at the nose. You got yourself a bad case a sunburn and delirium trimmins and jaundice. You all gone to yeller. Git in here with yer old true-blue friends, Horlick called.

But old Mommy, she just flung her newspaper hat into a

ditch and waved her bourbon bottle in a threatening gesture at a jeep filled with men in guerrilla costumes.

Stick 'em up! Mommy shouted. Hey waddy woo woo!

The last anyone ever saw of that soul were bits of newsprint from her newspaper hat floating over the Artibonite Valley, and long years later, in a village in the North, the Memphis needlepoint lunch-bucket pocketbook with the names of children and grandchildren doodled in red thread.

The horror of life's good jokes ending so abruptly, Horlick thought. Maybe it is time to go home. But they had no home. They had no place.

From the back of the car, where Sleep sat emitting soy sauce and ginger fumes and whiffs of garlic and happy clouds of bean paste and papaya, it occurred to the dog that the two H.'s had a tendency to drift. But enough was enough. Sleep, too, had reached an age that made him feel the need for an anchor, dear God, an anchor, and time to reflect. And decent eye drops.

Darlings, Sleep wheezed. My darlings.

That day, the dog took unto himself the glove compartment. That night, the delicious windshield wipers. Then the gearshift and the headlights.

He knew no rest.

He knew people, though.

He knew history.

He knew what he knew.

On a Sunday summer morning most memorable for its dazzling dew, the perpetual journey officially ended. In a far country, near the banks of a trickling river, what was left of the roving automobile became the medical missionary's roadside clinic for the dispensing of mud packs, birth-control pills, boiled flowers for headaches, hair powders, razor blades and string for the cutting of the umbilical cord, and a gradually acquired expertise in the setting of simple fractures.

Like the female evangelists in turn-of-the-century China,

those self-sacrificing and self-demeaning Victorian ladies who had also journeyed to foreign lands and who had become the Western she-tigers with the enormous hands and feet, Horlick and Horticulteur became upright, autonomous, fearless.

Nu chang fu, the Chinese had called the evangelists. Women walking among men.

Beside the river, under the shade trees, the roadside, clinic, medicine ball, She-tiger became a glistening and purposeful spot on the world's map, an island of calm for the poor and abused, a stopping-off place for a nuclear physicist with whom Horticulteur departed on the morning of her fortieth birthday, an oasis for scores of geologists and transit-authority officials and a family looking for orange drinks and, now and then, a river man.

On certain quiet afternoons, ditto the blessed answer to Sleep's dreams. **Q**

Chemicals

Craig could never fall asleep after sex. He always wanted to design a building, or cook a meal, or listen to records with the headphones on. His wife, Ellen, said Craig was a strange cookie. She said most men can't stay awake after sex. She said there's a chemical released in the brain that puts you to sleep. She said she read it in a magazine.

"I'm not a cookie," Craig would say.

Sometimes he would get out of bed and eat a sandwich or clean the apartment, but usually he would just lie there with his eyes open, listening to his wife breathe. He would have his hand on her belly.

One time he put some clothes on and went outside for a walk.

It had rained all day, and the sidewalks were still wet. There were worms all over the place. Craig tried not to step on the worms, but every now and then he would feel one under his shoe.

"I am not a worm," he said to himself. "I am a guy who can't sleep."

At the playground on Clark Street, a little fat boy was shooting baskets in the dark. He asked Craig if he wanted to play.

"How old are you?" Craig said.

"Nine," said the boy.

"Why are you up so late?" Craig said.

The kid just looked at him.

"I can't sleep," Craig said. He looked at the fat kid. He looked at how fat the kid was, and imagined the names the other kids must have called him: "Fatso." "Two-ton." "Porky." "States."

That's what the kid was doing at the playground in the middle of the night.

"Do you want to play, or what?" he said. He must have been half Craig's size, and Craig wasn't very tall himself.

"I'll play," Craig said.

They played and the fat kid walked all over him. The kid was fast and he could shoot. He shot inside and he shot outside. He slam-dunked it, jumping so high his feet were in Craig's face.

I've died and gone to sleep, Craig thought.

When they finished playing, the fat kid said, "You owe me twenty dollars."

Craig figured he owed the kid something, so he took him back to his apartment. He led the kid up the stairs and they took off their shoes outside the bedroom door.

Inside, Ellen was sleeping, breathing like you breathe when you're asleep. She was sleeping on her back, naked.

Craig took the fat kid's hand, put it on Ellen's belly and held it there for the count of twenty.

He figured they were even. But then the fat kid started to hyperventilate and Ellen woke up.

"Craig?" she said.

"Ellen," Craig said over the fat kid's wheezy siren. "You should see this kid play basketball," he said. **Q**

Flag of Hawaii

This is for the Captain, *ke Kapena,* may your heart rest in peace. Now no longer the bachelor, I can see you there on the altar, standing upon ship, looking over water, your Pacific, Oahu, a honeymoon awaits you beyond. May yours be simple, outdoors where God will overlook you, or look down upon you, or so as you may remember this is what we at one time appeared to have had agreed. The Father, the Son, the Holy Ghost, they are here with me. We salute you. Half-mast waves the flag of Hawaii.

Ahoy! Today is a day of mourning, a day to mourn a memory, the memorial of you, Captain, yours, of how I first saw you, you with your medallions of some adonis, an explorer who knew what he had come for. You, Captain, you knew what you had come here for. You came, you saw, you anchored my harbor, my God. The Virgin Mary witnessed this. May she be the virgin to christen your ship. Break a bottle on the bow, the stern, the altar. The bells of the buoys are ringing now.

This gift you gave, Captain, this that you called your bible, an atlas, what you wrote to me within remains. You say here how you love, dear, lovely, how you wish, want, yearn, how there is time and space, eternal. Here you, you Captain yourself, you say for me to please enjoy this gift of your love forever. How long is forever for?
Speak.
Now.

Captain, you spoke of your women as islands, every one of your women, an island, Hawaiian, divine. Your nights on Kauai and your wreck in Kahoolwe, your loss of Molokai and her sister Lanai, your longings for Maui and your hell with Hawaii, Oahu and you in her honolulu. These your women, Captain, they are drifting, they are drowning, they are falling overboard. Cast down the lifevests, the lifeboats, the oars. Your women are calling, Captain, calling you, Mayday and S.O.S.

He who fell before you, the late Captain James Cook, he was a Captain who followed the path of Venus around and around the world. Here in the world of Hawaii, your natives took him to be their God but, in the end, your same natives took his life. Death by a dagger, this Captain lie face down in the waters he himself claimed to have had discovered. Mercy falls upon you, Captain, no more tours around the world, no more greetings as God, no more harbors there to welcome you. Bless your blessed anchor, bless it now before you, Captain, for once it is lost, Captain, no one, not even yourself, can be saved.

Here, then, is where I leave you, Captain, as you yourself once left me. May your bride be the discovery, the island, to you who I never was. May you glorify her, your bride, sacred as the harbor, Pearl. May you comfort her through war and through peace, in victory and in defeat, past death to forever if ever never part. The Father, the Son, the Holy Ghost, we all of us bow our heads for this moment of silence, a moment of prayer, an amen, amen.

Hoist the flag!

Anchors away!

May God be with you on your ship. **Q**

Rosie and Della, Sandy and Bessie, Sister and Dinah

The flies have found her. All winter, the only flies were those dead in the cold of the windowsills. Now the cold has turned to warm, the days are longer, and flies tick the window glass. The windows are raised. The front door is held open by daughters bringing clean nightgowns and cake, by granddaughters afraid to come in and happy to go home. The flies land here, loop there, find her and the others rocking and dozing. A fly lights on the back of her hand and walks a blue vein. The flies circle the rocking Mrs. Podolski and Mrs. Hatch and Mrs. Keck. Flies light on her sleeping face. Susan keeps the flies from the lips. One lights on the nose. Susan waves that fly away, then soft-whaps a fly on the sofa with a rolled-up newspaper. The old woman comes awake.

"Flies," Susan says to her. "Just some flies. Go back to sleep."

Summers, when her and her grandmother and Tops the dog fought the flies, is where she goes: those summers of Granddaddy coming in hatted and dusty for his noonday meal. Granddaddy makes sure the screen door is closed tight so that no more flies get in. And still, somehow, more flies get in, get on: flies that are walking specks on the white of the basin where Granddaddy washes his hands, on the white of the crockery in the cupboard, on the white-painted walls and lace-trimmed curtains, on the black of the Graywood stove. There are flies on Granddaddy's noonday meal of chipped beef and cream gravy. There are flies on the blue stitching of the linen covering the buttermilk biscuits. There are flies in the melting brick of Brownie Girl's butter. There are flies that Tops the dog snaps up with a lick of his black chops. There are flies everywhere in the farmhouse, so that Grandmother says, "Claire, I will give you a penny for every twenty flies that you catch and bring me."

And after the last of the red-chipped beef and the buttered buttermilk biscuits, after the rice pudding with raisins she at first thinks are flies, after still-hatted Granddaddy has smoked his pipe and gone back to mowing the fields, she and Tops the dog stalk the kitchen. She sweeps down a fly with Grandmother's flyswatter. Tops eats the still-buzzing fly. Tops wants more flies.

"Grandmother," she says to Grandmother pumping water over the plates from the noonday meal, "Tops is eating my money."

And Grandmother says, "Claire, my girl, Tops is doing what Tops can."

And after her and Tops finish patrolling the kitchen, there is the sheeted dark and quiet of the parlor. There are flies there. There are flies on the sheeted sofa and chairs. There are flies on the piano keys. There are flies on the family photographs of the newborn, the baptized, the gone-to-school, the graduated, the married, the gone-to-war, the come-back-from-war, the once-living, the once-dying, the all-dead. The flies are stirred from those faces all dead before she was born. The flies come back.

Her and Tops go back through the kitchen and out to the closed-in porch. There are flies on the outside of the screen door's screen. There are flies too high up on the glass of the tall porch windows for her to reach. There are flies down in the porch window corners, flies already dead, the leftover meals of spiders. One by one, she picks the flies up by crooked wings and bent legs. One by one, she drops the flies in the dab of soap on Grandmother's cracked bone saucer. She shows Grandmother the twenty-two flies that Grandmother counts out. She reminds Grandmother these are the flies that Tops has not licked up and swallowed down.

And Grandmother says, "Claire Fagan, you will soon be as wealthy a girl as you are already rich."

And there are those summer mornings of fighting the flies when Grandmother says the kitchen is too hot. The heat of the kitchen will have Granddaddy sweating more than his work in the fields, Grandmother says. The heat of the Graywood stove will have Granddaddy sweating more than the horses, Pat and Young Ned, pulling the clacking wooden blades out in the fields, Grandmother says, and so Granddaddy's noonday meal is taken outside.

There, under the cool of the two pine trees, Grandmother floats a quilt down. Grandmother lifts the quilt back up before the quilt can touch the brown pine needles, then lets the quilt again float down.

The plates and pitcher of milk are handed over from out of the apple-picking basket. The knives and linen napkins are laid down. Grandmother sees the hatted coming of Grand-daddy. Grandmother uncovers the sliced chicken, the peas, the boiled potatoes, the rhubarb pie sprinkled with powdered sugar. Grandmother napkin-wipes away the droplets on the pitcher of Brownie Girl's milk. Tops, on the quilt at Grand-mother's feet, snaps at the flies and the yellow jackets.

Grandmother and Granddaddy and her take their time with the noonday meal. When they are done, Grandmother clears away the plates and lifts aside the pitcher so they can all lie out on the quilt. They lie there, on their sides, on their backs, in the creaking and sighing of the two old pine trees above. They lie there in the pine-needle smell. They lie there with Grandmother and Granddaddy holding hands. They lie there with Granddaddy talking farm talk up through the straw of his hat. They lie there with her easy-petting Tops. They lie there dozing until Tops rolls up and snaps at the buzzing of a big horsefly. Tops misses, tries again, misses again.

Later, after Granddaddy has gone back to the fields with Pat and Young Ned, after Grandmother has flapped the brown pine needles from the quilt, after Grandmother and her have gone inside and Grandmother has washed the plates and started supper, after supper is done, after all that and before her bedtime, her and Granddaddy do the last of the day's chores. Her and Granddaddy go out to the barn and to Granddaddy's calling Brownie Girl. The flycatchers swoop out from the loft of the barn, circle in the getting-dark sky, then swoop down and around her and Granddaddy. Granddaddy claps and calls for his good Brownie Girl. Granddaddy calls with his then-still-strong voice carrying over the pasture where Pat and Young Ned fly-shudder in their skin. Granddaddy's voice carries over the granite stone wall going up the hill, carries over and up and across the cleared land to the high pasture and to the bell-clanking of Brownie Girl coming. And there is her running to her chore of getting Granddaddy's milking chair. Granddaddy sets down his milking chair on the other side of the tie-up rail worn smooth by the neck rubbing of long-dead cows named Rosie and Della, Sandy and Bessie, Sister and Dinah. And now Dinah's Brownie Girl looks in, her Brownie Girl head big in the closeness of the barn.

And Granddaddy says, "Come on, Brownie Girl. It's me and Claire." And Brownie Girl slow-clanks her way into the dark of the barn and over to the tie-up. And Granddaddy, tipping his straw hat up with the resting of his head on Brownie Girl's side, goes to work milking. And while Granddaddy does the milking, she goes over near Granddaddy's workbench and looks at the long-handled screwdrivers lined up from smaller to larger. She looks at the sharp teeth of the saws in the last of the day's light coming in through the window over Granddaddy's workbench. She looks at the curling yellow chaff of flypaper slow-twisting in the last of the day's light. The flypaper is thick with flies, thick with the dead. She looks at the sticky curl of flypaper and listens to Granddaddy strip the warm spurts of milk from Brownie Girl. Brownie Girl's tail swishes up the flies to buzzing all around Brownie Girl and her and Granddaddy. The flycatchers swoop into the dark of the barn from the almost all-dark outside and ghost-

flap around Brownie Girl and her and Granddaddy. One fly-catcher, seeing what is left of the day's light in the window over Granddaddy's workbench, thumps against the glass.

"Granddaddy," she says.

Granddaddy keeps the one-two count of Brownie Girl's milk filling the bucket.

"Granddaddy," she says again.

The *strip strup* of the milking stops.

"Granddaddy," she says, "there is a hurt bird over here."

The flycatcher, beak open, lies still in the sawdust and wood shavings on Granddaddy's workbench.

She hears Brownie Girl's bell clank. She hears Brownie Girl's milk foaming in the bucket. She hears Granddaddy set the bucket aside. Granddaddy scrapes back his chair and comes over from out of the dark to the workbench. Grand-daddy takes the flycatcher into his hands and smooths the dark feathers down.

Granddaddy says, "Poor thing, it broke its neck."

And Granddaddy says, "Don't cry, Claire; it did not suffer long."

And there is the summer of fighting flies when Grand-daddy takes to his bed with the sickness in his throat, stays in his bed, suffers long.

There, in the upstairs of during the day, she hears Grand-daddy trying to cough out the sickness in his throat. She hears Granddaddy cough as she looks for flies in the upstairs hall. She swishes the flyswatter down the hall until coming to the open door of Granddaddy's room. The shades are drawn and the room is dark. Tops, on the bed at Granddaddy's feet, thumps his tail.

"Shhh, Tops," she says.

Tops quits thumping.

Granddaddy lies there gasping. Granddaddy lies there in the sheet that Grandmother has floated down cool and clean, then flapped up full and open, to again float down, to let float all the way down.

The wind creaks and sighs the two old pine trees outside Granddaddy's window. The wind lifts the drawn shade, letting her look at Granddaddy not wearing his straw hat, the first time she can remember Granddaddy not wearing his straw hat. The wind keeps the shade lifted. She looks at the blue veins clumped on the back of Granddaddy's hands. She looks at the rings turned around on Granddaddy's fingers. She looks at Granddaddy's closed eyes and open lips. She looks at Granddaddy's lips working as if trying to tell her and Tops something. She looks at the thinness of Granddaddy's face. A fly lights on Granddaddy's face. The fly walks across Granddaddy's cheek. The fly walks over to Granddaddy's lips, trying to tell her something. The fly is there on Granddaddy's lips when the shade flaps down and Granddaddy's room again goes dark.

She hears the drawn shade tapping against the wood of the windowsill. She hears Granddaddy gasping. She hears Granddaddy telling her. She hears Granddaddy telling her how she will join him beyond the waters of the Deerfield River flowing down below the farm. She hears Granddaddy telling her how she will join him beyond those waters, and how they will walk together up the hill, up through the summer-green pasture where Brownie Girl and Pat and Young Ned graze. She hears Granddaddy telling her how they will walk together once more, as if after chores, and how they will walk together to where Grandmother and all her others wait for her, to where she hears the welcoming drone of her dead. **Q**

Pogo

My sister, Karen, is coming tomorrow. I haven't seen her in like four, five years. I keep looking at this photo I have of my family, back from when I was in junior high. I swear we could have been in a TV commercial. There's my little brother, Pauley, and he looks so beautiful. He's retarded, but he doesn't have slanted eyes or drool. His eyes are green like Mom's, with Mom's long eyelashes, and he has Dad's dark curls. Pauley's smile is a little goofy, but that's because his teeth weren't all in. Maybe a year after that picture, they sent him away to the special school and we only saw Pauley on holidays. And there's Karen, with her glasses, looking serious and smart. But she was so pretty that I'll bet no one ever called her Four Eyes. I'm in the picture, too. I was just a kid, but I bet my tits were bigger back then, and my teeth looked great, not like now. The shit they got me on now, it just wrecks your teeth.

The animals are in the picture, too. At that time there were three cats. One was Rex, our old cat, and I'm not sure who the other two were. There were always cats coming and going. There were also dogs. Pogo and Baron. Pogo was our old dog. We got him either for my fifth birthday or for Pauley's first. It was an old argument. Baron was a German shepherd that Pogo brought home with him the time Pogo ran away. Dad said one dog was plenty, but Mom cried that she had always wanted a German shepherd. She said we could give Pogo away. Karen and I looked at Mom like she was crazy.

"That's obscene," Karen said. "Pogo is our dog."

"Your mother isn't serious," Daddy said.

But Mom was, only none of us knew it then.

The funny thing I remember about that picture is that nobody took it. Daddy had just bought one of those cameras with a release lever and a tripod. He had set up the shot and run back to the table. And we really *were* laughing, because it felt sort of funny the way he'd gotten back so quick and had just enough time to put his arm around Mom and lean over and kiss her cheek. But even then, there was that moment after the click when Mom pushed Daddy away.

Anyway, a few years later, Karen was working and going to college part-time, and she moved into an apartment a few blocks away with her friend Sarah. I was in my last year of high school. We were sitting around the kitchen, eating lunch with Mom, who was reading *The Village Voice,* which we had never seen her do before. Mom started asking Karen questions like "What does EIK mean in an ad for a two-room apartment?" and "What good neighborhoods in Manhattan are cheap?"

I saw Karen look at Mom, Karen's eyes squinty like an old lady's. "What do you want to know that for?" she asked Mom.

And Mom said, "Oh, nothing. It's just that I have a friend looking for a place."

I thought Mom sounded a little scared, the way she said it. Sometimes she sounded that way when she talked to Karen, like there was a secret code between them.

I said, "What friend?"

I really didn't mean anything. It was just that it was a surprise, because Mom didn't seem to have any friends.

"No one you know," Mom said, and then she went into her bedroom and closed the door.

Karen didn't say anything. She took a lump of sugar and put it between her teeth; then she took a long sip of tea. I could hear her sucking up the sugar. She had picked this up from our grandparents on Daddy's side. And the whole time she was staring at the bedroom door like she was Supergirl with X-ray vision.

"What's going on?" I whispered.

"Nothing," she said.

A couple of months later, right at dinner, my mother told my father that she had a lover and that she'd never loved my father and it made her sick when he touched her. My mother told my father that he smelled funny, that when they made love she imagined that he was a corpse sometimes, or a creature from another planet. After that, Mom didn't always come home at night, and she just stopped doing things around the house. It was weird, like there was this woman walking around and we thought that she was Mom, but it wasn't Mom, it was this woman who had always hated us.

Karen left town soon after that. She'd gotten a scholarship to a school in California, and her roommate found a studio in Manhattan. So Daddy moved into their old apartment. He said it was good because it was a two-bedroom and near the house, so Pauley could visit when he was home from the special school and I could stay over sometimes.

It was summertime. I had missed too many classes and failed gym, so I was supposed to go back to school in the fall and be what they call a super-senior. But I didn't think I was going back. I found this secretarial job at an import firm. They'd asked to see my diploma and I told them I didn't have it with me, so they'd given me a typing test instead and asked me a few questions, and I did okay, so they gave me the job. I had been seeing D.J. for a few months already. At first Daddy hated D.J., but then Daddy got so busy moving out and fighting with Mom that he seemed to forget about me. Mom didn't care much what I did. "Do what you want. Just don't bring that son-of-a-bitch home."

I don't know why my mother didn't like D.J. He wasn't fresh. He always called her Mrs. Kramer. He always said stuff like "I see you are looking as lovely as ever, Mrs. Kramer. Has anyone ever told you that green *is* your color, Mrs. Kramer?"

I guess Mom thought D.J. was goofing on her. But I don't think he was. I mean, I don't think D.J. knew half the time whether he was serious or not. Maybe Mom knew we partied. But anyway, at first after Daddy moved out, my mother didn't bother me much. I wasn't home a lot and she was with her new boyfriend most of the time. She used to come home to walk the dogs, or sometimes she'd tell me to be home by a certain time to do it, but that was all.

"They're your dogs," I'd say.

"It's my house," she'd say back.

Then Mom's boyfriend dumped her, so she just hung out at home most of the time, and she'd walk the dogs because there was nothing else for her to do. One day I was about to leave to see Dad, and Mom asked me how he was.

"He's fine," I told her. "His new girlfriend is great."

"She'll find out," Mom said.

Dad was also dating other women. On Mondays, he was taking a class at an adult school in Manhattan. The class was called "How to Survive after Your First Divorce." Anyhow, things started to get weird that summer. Like D.J. and I had been doing a lot of coke and maybe popping a little smack now and then, but all of a sudden there was all of this base around. He started really getting into it, so I got into it, too. And Mom was getting stranger. She'd always liked to move furniture around and rearrange things, but then it got like she couldn't stop. I'd come home from work and there'd be cabinets and bookcases out in the street, and inside, there'd be different cabinets and bookcases that she'd found in some thrift place or at a garage sale. Once, she woke me up at 3:00 A.M. because she wanted me to help her tear down the wall between the living room and the dining room. And I mean, it was a work night, too. Sometimes Mom would get all done up and go out and not come home. But I didn't know if she was seeing someone or just hanging out at bars, or what. Then one night D.J. stopped by with a few of his friends and we all started partying. Mom got in at maybe five in the morning and there were empty bottles, rolling papers, razor blades, vials, you name it, all over. We were just sort of all around in the living room, too high to mind.

Mom started yelling that we were a bunch of degenerate junkies. D.J. told her to chill out. He was really being good, trying to get her to calm down. He said, "Why don't you relax and have a beer, Mrs. Kramer? Don't worry about anything, Mrs. Kramer. Me and the other guests will be happy to help Jennifer clean up before we leave, Mrs. Kramer."

Mom kept screaming, said she was going to call the cops. I got really mad. I couldn't control my emotions the way D.J. could. I just started to yell, so my mother grabbed a lamp and threw it at me. Hit my shoulder, too. Then she ran into her room and slammed the door. Everybody, including D.J. and me, left. I stayed at D.J.'s for a couple of days. He told me I should apologize to my mother, maybe bring back flowers. So I got Mom a silk blouse from the import firm where I worked. But when I came home, she wasn't there. All my stuff was packed in two plastic garbage bags on my bed. I just looked at those bags and started to cry. I called D.J. to tell him I was moving in, but he started giving me this rap about how it would spoil our relationship.

"Come on, D.J., I need a place," I said.

D.J. said, "Yeah, but I'm talking about our love for each other. It's like this tantra stuff I'm reading. Look at your parents. I mean, I can't believe how selfish you're being."

I told D.J. I was sorry. I picked up the bags and dragged them the ten blocks over to Dad's. When I got there, Dad just looked at me for a while like he was thinking about what to say.

"Your mother said you two had some argument," he said.

"I don't know," I said.

Daddy kept hinting around about how small the apartment was, how the spare room was really for Pauley. He was beginning to remind me of D.J. He had a date that night. Before he left, he said to me, "Jen, I know you're a big girl now."

After Dad was gone, I looked in the refrigerator. There was just some cold Chinese food. The paper container was beginning to fall apart, and it smelled a little funny, but I ate it anyway. I thought of calling D.J., but I remembered the way he was. I remember wishing that Dad hadn't gone out. I sort of thought my first night there we could have had dinner together. I could have cooked something for him. When I was four and my sister was maybe eight, we made Dad dinner when Mom was in the hospital having Pauley. It was fun.

After I ate, I did a few lines, found a joint in my purse, and took a bath. It was weird, because I was living in Karen's old apartment. I never knew that it was going to become Dad's apartment and that Mom would have a lover or any of that.

Dad didn't say anything about me helping with the rent, which was good, because all my money seemed to be disappearing. It was party, party, party. I'd go into work some days, and my bosses, these two Pakistani guys, Mr. Bhu and Mr. Paul, they'd be asking, "Jennifer, you look so tired. Jennifer, what is wrong?" I started to tell them I had family problems. D.J. kept borrowing money, too. He said he knew some people. He said he could start dealing if he just got the capital together; make big money. Anyway, one night Dad and me were both sitting around the kitchen, and the phone rang and there was no one there. Then, about ten minutes later, the bell rang. It was Mom. She had Pogo with her. Pogo went crazy seeing us. He was pulling Mom up the steps.

"Hey, Poge! Hey, Poge!" I said.

He was jumping on me like I'd been gone for years.

Mom said, "I'm getting a job. I can't take care of him anymore."

Dad said, "We have jobs."

Mom said, "Look, you do what you want! I don't want him."

She dropped his leash and a shopping bag full of his dishes and toys. Then she left. Dad went after her, but Mom got into her car and drove off.

"Bitch," Dad said. "The bitch has the shepherd—she can take care of the shepherd, she can take care of him."

"Oh, come on, Dad, I can take care of him," I said.

Pogo was licking my face. I was really getting off on it.

I felt so responsible at first. I'd get up in the morning, walk the dog, eat breakfast, go to work. But I was beginning to get really edgy. I couldn't believe I was eighteen and my whole life was going to a job and walking a stupid dog. So I called up this friend of D.J.'s and went over. First we were just doing a few lines, and then he offered to cook up some base. He said he had some other stuff to mix in. It was really kind of sexy, the way he undid his belt and wrapped it around my arm, then pulled real tight. I screamed a little. He stroked my arm and told me I had beautiful veins. No shit, beautiful veins! He put like a quarter of it into me and the rest into him. Some of my blood was in his. He told me this meant we were related.

When I got back to the apartment, I just kept thinking that all I wanted to do was smoke a joint and take a nap. But as soon as I opened the front door, I heard this yelping from inside. And Mrs. Zerski from downstairs was coming out and she said, "Your damn dog's been at it since last night."

I ran up the stairs. Pogo jumped on top of me and I could smell the shit and piss from somewhere in the apartment. I figured Dad must have stayed out all night. Nobody had walked Pogo for a whole day. I cleaned up the mess and took him out. I didn't feel well. I felt kind of dizzy and tired, and I knew that I really needed to get something. It was scary because it was like the first time I knew I really needed.

When I got back, I put some newspapers around the spot where Pogo had done his business. He didn't even want to go near it. He kept his head down like he thought I was going to hit him. Then the phone rang. I felt so happy to hear D.J.'s voice. He said he had something special for us. I put out some food and water for Pogo, got some things together, and started to leave. Pogo followed me to the door. He actually left his dinner to follow me. I couldn't remember him ever leaving his food before. When I closed the door behind me, I could hear Pogo barking. He wasn't really as loud anymore. It was more like a whimper—like he knew it wouldn't do him any good to cry out, but he couldn't help feeling bad.

The next night, I came home and took Pogo out for a long walk. I walked down near Mom's house and I remember having this funny thought that if I went inside Mom's house,

Karen and Pauley and Dad would all be there and it would be the same again. It was a crazy feeling.

One day I came home from work and Pogo didn't even get up to say hello to me. He just stayed in a corner and looked at me like I was some kind of stranger.

"Tough shit, Pogo. We all got to make adjustments," I said.

I started to go out the door again and he started barking. I yelled at him to shut up. I felt like he was against me, that he was trying to lay this whole thing on me. And like if it wasn't for me, my mother would have taken him to the pound. He was being so ungrateful. I was really pissed. I moved my hand like I was going to slap him, and he bit me. The next day, Dad and I had a conversation about it.

"He's always barking at Bonnie," Dad said. Bonnie was Dad's new girlfriend. "I can't even bring her over to the house anymore."

"He's changed," I said. "Pogo's gotten mean."

"I asked your mother if she'd take him back," Dad said.

"What did she say?"

"She said we should have him put to sleep," Dad said.

We didn't talk about it after that. But things started to get worse. Pogo would shit in the middle of the living room, under my bed, anywhere but on the paper. You'd open the apartment door and he'd try to run out. He was always growling, making mean noises. And home wasn't the only place things were getting crazy. One Friday afternoon, I thought I was the last one left in the office. There was this whole shipment of silver jewelry from Pakistan. I was going to take a few bracelets. Just a few. D.J. figured we could sell them right out on the street. Only it turned out that Mr. Paul was there. He caught me. I started to cry. I told him my father beat me. I told him I needed money for a security deposit so I could get my own apartment. He kept saying, "Poor Jen-ni-fer. Poor, poor Jen-ni-fer."

He told me not to worry. He asked me how much I needed. I just made up an amount. Three hundred dollars. He took five twenties from his pocket and counted them out as he put them in my hand. Then he kissed me. He told me he would give me more. My father had gone upstate with Bonnie for the weekend. Mr. Paul drove me back to the apartment. When he came up, Pogo started snarling. I had to lock Pogo up in the kitchen. There's no door. I tied his leash around a riser.

The next weekend I spent at D.J.'s. When I got home, Dad was just sitting in the kitchen, smoking a cigarette. He looked kind of funny.

"What's wrong?" I said.

"Jen, I think we should do it," Dad said.

He made the appointment at the vet. The vet was way out on Queens Boulevard. Dad couldn't find a parking spot, so he just stopped and let me out. "I'll come in if I can find something," he said.

I didn't really want to go in alone, but I figured I'd have to wait awhile, anyway, and then Dad would catch up with me. But I hardly had to wait at all.

Pogo was scared. I was scared, too. I was afraid the doctor would say something to me. But he just asked me if I wanted to be in the room. I said, "Yeah."

It was like a regular doctor's office, except the table wasn't as long. The nurse, or assistant, whatever you call her, even had on a nurse's cap. We both held Pogo down. He was barking a little. I watched the doctor fill up the needle. My eyes closed when he came back to the table. I couldn't watch him do it. Pogo barked a little more. Then he just stopped. When I opened my eyes, I looked into Pogo's. They were like buttons on a stuffed dog.

Anyway, Daddy moved to Cincinnati with his new wife. I visited him out there once, but it was weird. My sister must have written him that I was here, because I got a letter from him last week. He said he would come as soon as things got settled in his new store. I can just see it. He'll make it up a few minutes after they cart me down to the icebox. He'll tell the doctor he was looking for a parking space. **Q**

DIANE WILLIAMS

Passage of the Soul

She said, "Don't get excited," to the scar-faced man.
He was excited, more like agitated. I remembered lots of
men I have been with being like that. It was a worry. Maybe
he was someone who shouldn't have been out.

She said, "We don't have to stay," and then I saw him in
the snack line, way behind me, stuck in the heavy crowd, from
where another woman's voice scolded somebody, "You had to
pick the most popular picture of all the pictures!" Next, I
found my husband. I always can. He goes ahead without me
for the seats.

We hardly speak in theaters, waiting. I twisted myself
around to watch a girl behind us feed her boyfriend one
popped kernel of corn, and then kiss him, and I saw him touch
her breast, because we had to wait and wait, even for the
previews to begin. I decided her boyfriend was no one I would
want touching from, and I didn't flinch; he did, when I watched
him watch me make my decision. It was as though he couldn't
believe it, that he couldn't believe it—that I would judge him
with such haste.

I would have run off with the character named Tom in the
movie, so that they could see once and for all, as he put it to
the woman, how they would be together, away from all of *this*.
She ended up unappealing. She must have had a moment of
horror—the actress—when she first saw herself like that.

At one time, seven years earlier in the movie, it seemed the
whole audience had heaved a huge sigh watching her—not me,
I just listened—I never would want to let on what I was thinking, You are so bold and lucky, when she dropped the pro-
phylactics into her purse before she went out, and I was eager
to see what would happen.

There are so many other things to recount about that

movie. I left the theater with our balled-up empty popcorn bucket in my hand, to throw it away at home: that's what I was thinking about on the way to our car, that I'd have to hold it in my hand, which I did, feeling it, the squashed-up waxy rim of the bottom of it, all the way home; that somehow I had ended up like this. I had missed, just to begin with, the opportunity to throw it away inside the theater.

When we were getting ready for bed, I got myself into sort of a state. I saw that my husband was wearing what I considered to be the trousers of my pajamas—I have only one pair —which I had planned to put on, which had belonged to him once long ago, it's true, but hadn't he given them to me?

"What do you think you're doing?" I asked him. "I don't get it. What are you doing?"

I saw him, his body, his bare chest, which is sleek and perfectly formed by my standards—he was pulling down and folding the spread of our bed, in those cotton striped trousers. My husband is so graceful, how he moved around the foot of the bed was so graceful, how he gently, carefully folded.

Oh, he gave me back the trousers; so then we slept.

I didn't know what the issue was.

When the ringing of the telephone woke us in the night, we both knew what it could mean—everybody does—or it could have been just somebody borderline, wanting to hear the sound of anyone in a fright. *That's* what it was that time.

More will happen.

It will be stunning.

It's what I'm waiting for.

Some people, they are lucky—just walking, just going around, when you look at them. **Q**

Baby

Nobody was getting up close to me, whispering, "Do you get a lot of sex?" Nobody was making my mouth fall open by running his finger up and down my spine, or anything like that, or talking dirty about dirty pictures and did I have those or anything like those, so I could tell him what I keep—what I have been keeping for so long in my bureau drawer underneath my cable-knit pink crew—so I could tell him what I count on happening to me every time I take it out from under there. Because it was a baby party for one thing, so we had cone paper hats and blowers, so we had James Beard's mother's cake with turquoise icing, and it was all done up inside with scarlet and pea-green squiggles, and the baby got toys.

Nobody was saying, "Everybody has slept with my wife, because everybody has slept with everybody, so why don't we sleep together?" so I could say at last, "Yes, please. Thank you for thinking of me." I would be polite.

Just as it was nothing out of the ordinary when the five-year-old slugged the eleven-year-old on the back and they kept on playing, looking as if they could kill for a couple of seconds. We didn't know why the five-year-old had slugged the eleven-year-old. And then the baby cried in a bloodthirsty way.

My husband sat stony-faced throughout. I don't think he moved from his chair once. What the fuck was wrong with him? He left the party early, without me; he said to get a little—I don't know how he was spelling it—I'll spell it *peace*.

I spoke to a mustached man right after my husband left. He was the first man all night I had tried to speak to. I know he loves sports. I said to him, "I think sports are wonderful. There are triumphs. It is so exciting. But first, you have to know what is going on."

Then my boy was whining, "Mom, I want to go home." He was sounding unbearably tired.

The baby's aunt said she'd take us. She didn't mind. She had to back up her car on the icy drive. She said, "I don't know how we'll get out of here," when we got into the car. "The windows are all fogged up." She said, "I don't think I can do it." She opened the window and poked her head out. She said, "I don't think so."

When she closed the window, we went backwards terrifically fast. I don't know how she knew when to spin us around into the street. It was like being in one of those movies I have seen the previews for. It was like watching one of those faces on those people who try to give you the willies. It was like that, watching her—while she tried to get us out.

It was so exciting.

Goo-goo.

Fucking goo-goo. **Q**

Killer

Past the shimmering gewgaws on the velvet shoes at N-M, I went on by them, chasing two women, especially the one in the raccoon coat, who is glamorous—Marlene—my neighbor's new third wife—he had to have—a divorcee with five children, a convert from Catholicism for him for love—I was on her side. They are all so devout.

I adore I adore I adore—she should have said, I love only you, when she took what I had to give her away from me, because the sunglasses on the counter where I had just paid for my lunch might have been hers, and they *were* hers! She said something ecstatic and I hardly had to do anything, except ride back down the escalator, past pricy purses, veering nearly into jewels, and then into the jewels, where I said no, then on out the huge doors of N-M. I needed to go along over the black pavement, stamping and looking, and, bingo, with my instinct, I would see my car. Postponing the joy of getting into it, for what I would be doing next, I stood and took in the air, and looked around at so much air.

You know how it can hug you and kiss you all over because it is all over you anyway, and inside of me, and I was out there like a smoker—not to try to smother my lungs—just to have something to do with my fingers, and with my hands, and with my mouth, pressing them up against absolutely nothing at all, or aiming to get through it, when there is not a human being I know of who wants to do it with me, my feelings are hurt, when all they would have to do is bat their eyes at me and I would consider myself half the way there.

He doesn't have to stand on his head. Who cares what he does? I think my luck will hold for me. Yesterday they picked up Squeaky Fromme—two men did, after her breakout out of jail. Her being wanted, it didn't go on overly long. **Q**

The Nature of the Miracle

The green glass bottle rolled into, rolled out of, my arms, out of my hands, and then exploded, just as it should, when it hits our bluestone floor, and spreads itself, and sparkling water, on the territory it was able to cover from our refrigerator to the back door.

The bottle used to fit tightly in my hand, easily, by the neck, and the way one thing leads to another in my mind, this means I should run away from my marriage.

I should run to the man who has told me he does not want me. He does not even like me. Except for once he took me, and my head was up almost under his arm, my neck was, and my hand went up his back and down his back, and he copied what I did to him on my back with his hand, so that I would know what it would be like, I would have an idea, and then I could run home to my marriage afterward, which is what I did before, after we were done with each other; and the way one thing leads to another in my mind, this means I should run to the man for more of it, but the way one thing leads to another, first I will tell my husband, "I would not choose you for a friend," then I will run to the other man, so that I can hear him say the same thing to me.

This is unrequited love, which is always going around so you can catch it, and get sick with it, and stay home with it, or go out and go about your business getting anyone you have anything to do with sick, even if all that person has done is push the same shopping cart you pushed, so that she can go home, too, and have an accident, such as leaning over to put dishwasher powder into the dishwasher, so that she gets her eye stabbed by the tip of the bread knife, which is drip-drying in the dish rack. It is a tragedy to lose my eye, but this heroism of mine lasted only a matter of moments. Q

Forty Thousand Dollars

When she said forty thousand dollars for her diamond ring, where did I go with this fact? I followed right along with her, hoping, hoping for a ring like hers for myself, because of what I believe deep down, that she is so safe because she has her ring, that she is as safe as her ring is big—and so is her entire family—her husband who gave her the ring, all of her children—and no one has ever tried to talk me out of believing this fact, because I would never talk about it, that the entire quality of her life is totally secure because of the size of that ring—that the ring is a complete uplift—that every single thing else about her is up to the standard the size of her ring sets, such as even her denim espadrilles, which I love, which she was wearing the day she was talking to me, or her gray hair pulled back, so serene, so that she is adored, so that she is everlastingly loved by her husband, and why not?—just look at her! —and she is loved by her children, and by everyone like me who has ever laid eyes on her and her ring.

She was waggling it, which I loved her to do, because I loved to see it move, to see it do anything at all, and she said, "I make my meat loaf with it." She said, "I like that about it, too," and I saw the red meat smears she was talking about, smearing up the ring the way they would do, the bread all swollen up all over it, all over the ring part and the jewel. I saw my whole recipe on that ring.

She said, "It goes along with me to take out my garbage, and I like that," and I saw what she meant, how it would take out the garbage if it were taking it out with me, how it would go down with me, down the steps and out the back door—the ring part of the ring buried in the paper of the bag—and the dumping we would do together of the bag into the sunken can, before the likelihood of a break or a tear, or maybe I'd have to step on top of a whole heap of bags that was already down in there and then stamp on the top of the heap myself, to get it all deep down, to get the lid on with the ring on.

She said, "I never knew I was going to get anything like it. All that Harry said was, 'We'll need a wheelbarrow for you *and* the ring when you get it.' A wheelbarrow!" she said. "But now don't worry," she said to me. "You'll get one someday, too. Somebody will die," she said, "then you'll get yours—" Which is exactly what happened—I never had to pay money for mine, and mine ended up to be even bigger than hers. "This much bigger—" I showed her with two fingers that I almost put together, the amount, which is probably at least another carat more, but mine is stuck inside an old setting and cannot be measured. That was the day I walked behind her, that I showed her, that I walked with her to her car when she was leaving my house.

The rings were of no account outside, when we were saying goodbye, when we were outside my house going toward the back side of her car, because we were not looking at the rings then. The heels of her denim espadrilles, which matched her long, swinging skirt, were going up and down, so was her strong ponytail, and her shoulders, and I wanted to go along with her to wherever she was going.

And the sense I had of not being able to stay behind her —of not being able to see myself in my own clothes walking away—the sense I had that I was not where I was, that I could not possibly follow in my own footsteps, was gone. Q

The Hero

My aunt was telling me about them coming to get them after I brought back the second helping of fish for me and the vegetables she asked for—the kind that have barely been cooked, that look so festive, even with the film of dressing that dulls them down. I didn't want her to have to get up to get her own, not since she's been sick.

My aunt was saying, "They're going to get us. Hurry! Hurry! They're going to kill us!" after I put the vegetables down for her.

She said, "Your mother was a baby in my mother's arms." She said, "I get out of breath now when I eat. Jule says I'm not the same since I was sick. He says to me, You've changed."

"You haven't changed," I said.

She said, "They had the wagon loaded. They had the cow. You know they had to take the cow to give the children milk to drink. They were going to hide! To hide! To hide in the woods! And then Jule said, I've got to go!

"Everything was loaded. They said, Hurry! They're coming! They're going to kill us! But Jule said, I've got to go! So they said, Do it! Do it! Hurry! So then Jule said, But I need *the pot!*"

"He said that?" I said. "I never heard that story. Does my mother know that story?"

My aunt smiled, which I took then to be no. And my mother wasn't there, so I couldn't rush to her, I couldn't tell her, Do you know the story about your family? How you were going to be killed? How Uncle Jule stopped everything to go?

Uncle Jule appeared then. He was wearing a white golf hat.

My aunt said, *"You could put it in your hat."*

She said that to Jule.

I don't remember why she said that—*You could put it in your hat.*

He must have said something first to her about her vegetables—could he take home what she wasn't going to eat? Maybe that was it—but it doesn't matter.

Uncle Jule was blinking and smiling when she said, *You could put it in your hat.* He was blinking faster than anyone needs to blink.

Cauliflower was what my aunt left on her plate. It looked to me like some bleached-out tree. **Q**

Mystery of the Universe

The five-year-old sitting at the head of the table said, *"Think!* You're not thinking. *Think!"*

So I tried to think, because he had said I had to.

"It has something to do with the angel," he said.

We all looked up at the lit-up Christmas tree, to the top, where I saw it pressed into the wooden beam, something golden and bent. The question, the child's question, was "What made the roof cave in?"

"He changes the rules when you start to guess it," his ten-year-old brother said.

It was true. I remembered his first hint—"It has something to do with the train," which was on tracks at the base of the tree.

The size of the child's forehead, of his whole head, is astonishing for anyone of that age, for a child of any age, for any person—the breadth and the depth and the length of it—and then at dinner it was full of the question.

"You're not thinking!" he said again. *"Think!"* when I said that the top of the tree had pushed through the ceiling, had made the ceiling cave in, and I am forty-two.

"No!" he said. *"That's not it!* Who can guess what it is?"

There were two families together, guessing while we were eating. He wasn't my child with this question, but I wished that he were. He is a child to be proud of, who would force us to think, who would not let up. I didn't mind that he'd stoop to being sneaky. I was proud of him. I am proud of anyone who stands up to everyone, who would say it to everyone in front of everyone—*"You're the kind of person who would pull out a tree out of our front yard and throw it down on the house!"* I was so proud of a person who would think of doing the scariest thing he could think of, and he isn't even Jewish. **Q**

The Composer

The phone is dead. Tracy knows the phone is dead but will reach for it in the middle of a brainstorm and start to dial before he remembers: dead air. Then he feels like a fool again. Tomorrow, phone service will begin in his new apartment. Today, he keeps weighing the mute instrument in his palm.

His six-year-old is more comfortable with phones than he is. He suspects generally that she is more comfortable in his presence than he is in hers, which amazes him. He still expects Thea to be a shy child. He selects topics of conversation en route to the house from work and presents them prematurely at the door. Thea's remedy is to suggest he have a glass of water. Thea is big these days on prescribing glasses of water; her world is a little theme clinic. This morning, moving day, Tracy called her from one of the phone booths outside the Mayfair Market, crazy to hear her voice, waited through four, five rings in the stuffy booth with his back to the sun when at last Thea answered. He overreacted: *Darling, it's Daddy.* She was baffled, silent. Tracy began smacking the mouthpiece with the palm of his hand. Thea thought it was a game and went overboard with it herself, *bam! bam! bam!* until Suzanne broke it up. "I'd like to get the kid to school," she told Tracy. He heard the ice cube rattle in her glass. "It's a crime to waste a brain."

The unpacked boxes terrify him. The first thing he locates is his electric keyboard, planted like a staff in a bed of loose orchestra charts. Then he finds his piano stool, but the place where he wants to put it down is blockaded by boxes. By first budging the boxes inch by inch, then rotating the chair around the new corners of the obstruction, he makes his way to the wall that will be his work space and lays the keyboard flat on the wood floor. He stares at it, waiting for the work space to come to life, but it won't. He tacks to the wall a page of notes to himself, the same one that was tacked to the wall of the old house. It feels dishonest to tack up a page of thoughts you thought someplace else, but he does it anyway. When he stares at it, though, it seems centered too carefully, lost from the bulletin-impulse that stuck it to a wall originally. Tracy removes the thumbtack and takes another stab, a little more offhand this time. Sunlight is coming in through the trees outside the window to make splotches on the wall that move back and forth evenly. It reminds Tracy of nothing, no place he's been. Unless he concentrates only on the hardness of the light; then he can almost get a hangover effect out of it, that bloodshot attitude he once liked in the mornings with Suzanne. He tries to reinvent it by squinting partway, but the scene seems to need one piece more.

It keeps needing one piece more: first the bed half unmade, later the magazines let drop to the coffee table from eighteen inches, in a gesture. All of this motivates Tracy to unpack and position every scrap of his belongings in under three hours. The apartment manager, who is named Vinny, declares that it's some kind of a record. "I'm flabbergasted," Vinny says, grinning from the doorway with his arms outstretched. He looks as if he is waiting to catch a medicine ball that he cannot see coming. Tracy bursts out laughing, much too loud to pass for good nature. But Vinny is not really paying attention. He looks instead at the memos on the walls. He points to the keyboard and says, "Yours?"

It bothers Tracy that Suzanne drinks every day and still gets things done, while he is sober and does not. He calls her a drunk and she bats her eyelashes. In any case, to her it's just another thing a person can be, another option with consequences. She told him once there are no penalties in life that haven't been discovered already. "You really seem to have your hands full *not* drinking," she added.

This is unfortunately true. He will not smoke or drink at

the keyboard, for one thing, and he often sits lockjawed there, resenting the walls and the hum of the machine. The image seems so pathetic to him now—and his moral posturings toward Suzanne so suddenly irrelevant—that he wants to cry, but only drops his head like a puppet-dancer who is waiting for the tune to start. It does not.

Paradoxically, living alone inhibits him. Tracy had moved to his first solo apartment a couple of years before he met Suzanne. It was in one of those narrow, double-decker West L.A. buildings that seem to have been swiveled away from the street upon completion. A childhood friend helped Tracy get all his things inside, but made his exit before the bookshelves went up. It was Tracy's idea to have two layers of shelving run up high along two continuous walls, connecting catty-corner by I hinges and fastened to the wall by brackets. The concept seemed to owe its design equally to the forms of aerodynamics and of pie cases. The friend was tremendously skeptical. Tracy reminded him of their success in constructing elaborate backboard apparatuses above driveways when they were growing up, and the friend responded that there were going to be similarities.

It took Tracy until after 2:00 A.M. to get the contraption up and on its own. Then he climbed on the back of the couch to load books onto the shelves—it had not hit him until now that the act of getting a book down from there was going to be equally impractical. It was too late to do anything about that. He made two even levels of books stretch the wingspan of the shelves, and then stood back to admire it all, dizzy with the strains of his own mind-music. He shut out the light and staggered to bed. Around nine, he awoke with the knowledge that the shelves would not hold. He had dreamed of fingers stretching membranes of sky. Delirium remembers the earth. He was on his feet even before he heard the walls complain. The unit was slipping on both sides. Tracy leaped up on the couch to support it from the middle, temporarily freeing either arm to bail out books from the sides. Chunks of the wall popped out like Styrofoam, and at last Tracy had to make a break for it. He hurled himself to the center of the floor as the shelving dropped straight as a chute. The doorbell rang, and in came the man from the phone company, stepping over splintered planks to find the outlets.

Tracy wonders if his victimization by phones is the penalty for not understanding how they really work. If a device is chiefly supernatural to you, then anyone can throw a whammy on it. He sets his keyboard on its stand, hunches over it in the lamplight. He aches for his wife and daughter tonight. He decides that he is hexed, wonders how the walls withstand it —all the slashing red-and-blue sounds he hears beyond them seem to encircle. He opens the window to reassure himself that the noise is something he understands; it's the Hollywood Freeway, as a matter of fact.

Suddenly, though he could not draw from the phone a sense of closeness to Suzanne, the Santa Ana winds and the night air give him one. It was back when they first noticed each other at the stage company. She worked in the box office and borrowed money from everyone on the crew before her first week was up; he was trying to quit cigarettes, and slipping— each of them began unsuccessfully to ask the other for a smoke. She got a kick out of him and told him that whenever they did have a cigarette together, it was going to be *something*. After that she just whispered "something" every time they passed in the hall. He bought the first pack.

What he sees now are her legs. She had just lifted herself onto the bookkeeper's desk in the front office, where Tracy sat drinking from a half-gallon carton of milk. It was six o'clock and they were the only two left in the place—everyone had made a point to be out of the neighborhood before the Holly- wood Christmas Parade began. Now the streets were closed. Tracy was probably the only person in the company who had not known about the Hollywood Christmas Parade, and Su- zanne was definitely the only one who knew and forgot. She drank from his milk carton and did pixie motions with her legs, a parody of an office girl. She had newsprint on her nose. "Listen to my legs," she had said.

Listen to the legs. Tracy curses. He does not look at things any longer the way he looked at Suzanne's stockinged legs. Suddenly this seems significant, even occult. Caught up in the weight of the legs, the lay of the legs on the desktop, is his ability to experience again, to have back the wind and the desire and the parade and everything supernatural; to feel anything without feeling instantly the loss of it. Something about the legs. He decides to try to sketch them—reaches for a pencil and closes the keyboard for a tabletop.

She had laughed, half choking on the milk. He played with an RTD map and pointed out all the places he was going to take her. Then he let her look at it herself while he put her in slow poses on the desktop, positioning her shoulders and tugging at her lip. Her eyes kept misting over, as though she were suppressing a sneeze. Most likely she was drunk.

Tracy is quickly irritated that he has never learned to draw. Nevertheless, he arrives at an intuitive technique, based on the notion that if you mark up the page liberally enough, some of it will begin to remind you of the thing you intended to draw, and then you will build on it. When you drew like Tracy, you primarily had to be alert. Now he sketches, assesses, erases. Each pang of recognition thrills him on to the next one, until the legs begin to look real. Frighteningly real at first. And then there is a turning point, an instant in which he knows that his vision is no longer necessary, that the drawing is independent —a moment of satisfaction so true it cannot be trusted.

For the drawing has begun to look too real, too literal; it has begun to resemble a drawing. It has supplanted the memory. Tracy stares at it but cannot make it come to life. Under the orange, irrational lamplight, the legs he sees are as good as pressed. Of course he cannot "listen to them." He cannot even remember what he wanted them to do.

What did I want them to do, Tracy repeats, wishing into the page.

"Holy cow. It is cold in here."

Tracy is too possessed to realize that what is happening is real. Vinny has opened the door with a passkey and marched past Tracy to the window. "You wanted this window open?" Vinny says, before closing it.

"Tracy." The voice is Suzanne's. She is walking toward him, dizzy as usual, but as cautiously as if he were armed. He shuffles the drawing aside and she stops, puzzled. Her hair is in her eyes. She looks at the walls, the work space, and her mouth drops. "Oh, Jesus, it's the same," she says.

"You people don't think it was a little cold in here, for God's sake?" Vinny says. He turns his palms out to Tracy. "So how come you can't answer the door?"

Suzanne moistens her lips. "He looks so fuckin' flushed," she says with her smeary smile, then conks herself on the forehead. "Shit, what a thing t'say." She backpedals to sit on the bed and misses.

Tracy knows that Thea is staring at him from the doorway, but he cannot look up. He sits warily, breathing through his nose, unable to find a spot in the room where he can rest his eyes.

Suzanne gets up. "Figure I wait a decent interval, everyone forgets I fell." She nods brightly, waiting for Tracy to laugh first, then gives up on him.

Nobody else has moved. Now Suzanne paces the floor. Her high heels detonate on hardwood. She makes it to the stereo. "What are we, the Gestapo?" she says finally. "He doesn't want visitors."

It is well past midnight when Tracy pushes himself away from the keyboard. But if he thinks about it hard enough, it could be 5:00 P.M., maybe 6:00. So long as you agree it's winter, 5:00 and midnight look the same. Suzanne would be arriving with Thea any moment. They would perhaps have been buying groceries. Tracy would be standing right here, by the furnace, having arrived just ahead of them with the newspaper. (He grabs a newspaper.) Of course, nobody has cleaned the place. And Thea's coloring book on the couch would be open to any page, the final detail—only Tracy doesn't have anything resembling a coloring book.

He scans the room.

He takes the phone off the hook to think. **Q**

Underneath Bridges Only a Walk Away
from Town

If it had been me and I had wanted to stay local for
the paper and all, the last place I think I would have chosen
was the cars-only, one-car-at-a-time, horn-as-you-come, red
wooden bridge that has the roof on it and the railings that are
thick-wide for kids' sneaker-feet when the kids climb up
against local law, as they always do, their standing in their
cut-from-jeans shorts, arms stretching for the hands-steadying
hold on the sidebars that hold up the roof, looking down to
what there isn't to jump into—rocks on rocks, most of which
are the size that could fill the craters on the moon, and weeds
growing from out from between the rocks and up along the
shore, where sure there is grass, but not much, and less so
flowers, not having much water I guess to grow on, since the
river is more of a stream than a river, and it was clear blood
that day of water when she had to go and jump off that bridge,
MaCreek's Bridge, as it is known around town.

About her choosing that bridge, I cannot help but think—
and maybe I am biased, but meet me the person who is not—
that she really wanted to use some other bridge, her being
born and raised here and therefore having to know the word
about on MaCreek's Bridge, it being the only damn-near-
haunted bridge in the whole county, recorded in the papers as
such, people from the West coming to stand on it and leaving
not believing, like most of our own kids, until the day after
something like her happens or until the hunters come home
early, not with rifles in their hands or with meat strung over
their shoulders, but with their dogs in their hands and their
rifles empty on their backs, their faces full-bruise-swollen from
the fights that they had had with each other after they had
taken turns holding down each other's dogs for the bullet-
square-shoot to the forehead that each master had to give to

his loving dog, because the bitch had ripped from her master's hold on the collar, or from even the whole dog sometimes, and gone barking-wild down in the direction of MaCreek's Bridge, where coming up through the trees was a glare-blowing, sting-leaf light that Pastor Whisser says is the Devil assuming God's holy-hallelujah form, and that the hunters say you do not want to turn your eyes away from, although you get the closest feeling you ever want to have of not being able to see, and when the dogs do come back, in the haze of cotton which you are left seeing, they are what else but blind dogs come back, walking mainly with their weight on their front paws, their hind legs paralyzed straight up from behind their joints, as if the dogs were circus dogs taught to do a one-dog wheelbarrow, and the hunters, although they try to bend their dogs' legs back underneath their bodies, can do nothing of the sort, except to make their dogs worse sometimes, by cracking a joint open, and to send them where the hunters say—with mouths open and chew-laughing laughs—that if they had had the choice of sending their dogs or of sending their wives, they would have sent their wives, since we all know a woman is easy to come by, but a hunt dog with a nose comes once in a life.

Took some talking, but Pastor Whisser is the best talker we have in town; educated in talk up city as he was in some fancy-spancy school, none of the like of which we have got around here, the Pastor talking the hunters into letting his wife, Dora, cut apart their dogs, the heads and legs of which, instead of being proper buried along with the other parts of the dogs, were instead prayed over and anointed in oil and ash by a pastor come over from the next county special. Some of the dogs' heads were pushed onto poles that had been wrapped many-men-high with flowers taken from along the shore underneath MaCreek's Bridge, flowers strung flower to flower to make vines of flowers used to offset the smell of dead dog and to lure your eyes up the poles, which the Pastor had shoved sun-dead center into the ground outside of chapel, so that wherever you were, you could see the poles rising to the chapel roof, to just below the wooden-laced roofed room where the bells are kept, the bells that call chapel, and you could feel the poles from wherever you were pulling you tall to the dead burned eyes of the dogs. To have seen from out of those eyes, what that would have been, a sin, Pastor Whisser said, and the smoking away of your eyes. Our kids took their chances anyway, climbing up the poles, getting only so far, never to the top, their feet soon caught in the vines, and the Pastor leaving the kids there for days on end, his ever-to-be-remembered lesson in the mercy of the Lord keeping safe our kids from the Devil. The kids not quite themselves after, quiet and fast-willing to be held by the ankles on the railings of MaCreek's Bridge to hammer into the sidebars—cross-boned style—the few dogs' heads that were remaining and all of the dogs' legs, the heads and legs becoming a part of the very bridge itself, even getting later almost that color the bridge gets when the sun is right low over in between the hills that surround our town, the heads and legs glowing in that way from what seemed to be their own light, showing us that Pastor Whisser had actually done—should there have been any doubt?—what with his words and his fire that day underneath the bridge he had promised us he was doing—conjuring up the Lord with the fire, asking the Lord to put a little piece of Himself into the heads and legs to make them alive in Him again and able to speak to the Devil, warn him to stay clear off our bridge and the hell out of our town.

The Devil seemed to heed the warning until the starlings, so set upon the heads and legs from the first that some say it was only God's will fighting against the will of the Devil that had kept the heads atop the poles and the heads and legs tacked to the bridge for as long as they had been, way past the time of rot, the bones slipping down the vines of flowers to within spinning reach of the bigger kids, and hanging clear from off the bridge, making the kids think that a bunch of them jumping together could knock off the bones—no go—the heads and legs staying put, like I said, way past the rot, the rotting you could taste in the air, in your soup at night, in the breath of the townswomen, each clutching a baby to her throat, as they went on with each other, right outside of chapel, so that Dora would hear and come on to the window, or to the inner screen of the door, or come on out, she the wife she is, the townswomen getting on her about the bone dust that was getting into their babies' throats, their babies' minds, to cause, the townswomen did not know what, but something, they were certain of that, something. Some disease in their babies, which Dr. Samuels would not find out about until only too late, their babies not able to be cured and dying before having babies of their own, no grandchildren, and the whole population going to naught, and all for what, the townswomen wanted to know, for that Pastor Whisser being stubborn and refusing to take down those poles. The townswomen like this on Dora every day, until when the Pastor finally hacked down the poles, saying how he was doing this for his people, but how he did not know, God bless His heaven for him to know, what now was to come of the poles not having been left in long enough to ward off the beast of the Devil once and for all, the Devil now able to come on in with even more even ease than before, and be he blamed, O Lord, blame me and not my people, for the soon coming of the Devil.

Come the Devil did. The bones that had been hanging from off the wood of the bridge for such a time suddenly dropped, to break below in pieces large enough for the kids to find, shine, and sell to the other kids next county over as magic-spell charms once used by the trolls, who, it is said, built all of the bridges, way eons ago, out of lamb and antelope hide, as protection against the dinosaurs, who just loved to eat them trolls. That is, that was, the kids said, before the trolls took down the clouds and molded the clouds with the heat of their bodies into the hard, stone-like, magic-spell charms, which the kids said they now held in their hands and which we could own for a fiver or for a stick of gum, charms so powerful, the kids said, they turned the dinosaurs into the rocks underneath the bridges only a walk away from town.

Because the Devil has settled on back into town and because of what the hunters tell is true is why I would not have gone near MaCreek's Bridge for want of death. Why I believe that that girl, name of Missy Janie, wanted to use some other bridge, such as the bridge way up over the Moosha River that everybody knows she loves, the rope swing being there, hanging down almost, but not quite, within reach of the bridge, making the rope swing the had-to-be-tried, the-swing-of-a-life —that slipping dropping inside your body and are-you-going-to-be-able-to, Christ-please-make-me-able-to, hold on, for that fly-through-the-air and that breaking-wind-skin in the cooling come breath of water, which overtakes your body as all those cheers from those barely-able-to-be-seen back on the bridge overtake your mind, you there in water—Missy Janie describing it in such that way and trying it herself many a time, any chance she had, her whistling a two-fingers-in-the-mouth whistle each time before she broke water, her way of telling her body, she said, that it had not ripped through its skin to land burning on the sun. That whistle that only Missy Janie could do—although she tried to teach us—could be heard above all the others as your legs kept you there in the water, arm awaving that you-are-all-right and for the next lucky one to come-on-at-it, to swallow the taste of water, next one after me always being Missy Janie, our planning it that way, so that I was one of ones, one of the two kids who was waiting back on the shore to help pull Missy Janie from out of the water.

Once she was out, the other kid who had helped, he headed back on for the bridge to wait his turn again, leaving me and Missy Janie alone to each other, to wait for the kid we were to help, me at Missy Janie with the arch-sloping, calf-length leaves that rushed in a trample down to the river, leaves of the lily plant, I think they were, without lily flowers anymore, these flowers having been torn off to be found later on the bottoms of our feet, petals blackened, yet still white-soft, as Missy Janie was to me then, in the shadowed rain of light banding through the trees that ran along the river, her in laughing movement, with her hands pushing away the leaves as they touched her body, and her finally giving in, sitting down in the shore grass in defeat, uncle, defeat, she said, as I went all over her body with the tips of the leaves.

When I sat down next to her, not giving enough between us but for one of us—me—to lay my arm flat on the shore, she was looking at I-don't-know-what, or where, but not at me, causing me to swim down inside my body, into my hips, to look at her from that far away inside, she a dream-of-a-girl feeling, nothing real to me, as she began rubbing her breasts, saying how the cedar water made her itch, and did it do that to me, too? and her turning to me, bringing me to float in my eyes, as she let me feel the wet hairs that grew between her breasts, such hairs on a girl I had never seen, let alone felt before, the hairs of men, which, Missy Janie said, were the surest sign of any that she knew that the Devil had marked her as his very own girl.

Maybe so, since we in town believe, led on in our believing by the Pastor Whisser himself, that Missy Janie, after finding that bridge way up the Moosha River kid-full, set on back to town, with the thought of finding some other bridge, but before she could come upon another one to her liking, the Devil, hearing her one voice, called to her, as he is apt to do, in a voice she took to be that of her own, leading her on to MaCreek's Bridge, where then the Devil stole her eyes—he always in search of the eyes he will wear over top his own when he comes to this earth in human form—and then he stole her legs—burning them in the ever-blackening fires to shape them into the canes he uses to beat the souls of hell—the Devil giving to Missy Janie in return legs that, although they looked like legs, could not move as legs move, Missy Janie left there beneath the bridge, waiting for who knows who finally finding her, dogs probably, and everybody in town claiming he or she had, Missy Janie with her arms blood-broken open and stretched way back over her head, as if she were waking in a morning-wake-the-body stretch, or as if she were reaching behind her for something, a pair of hands to take hold of her and pull her backward from off the rocks and from out of the water where she lay, body-dead, yes, but mind, oh, mind-alive.

Missy Janie was brought into town strapped down to a board lifted onto the shoulders of the hunters, their dogs alongside of them, running, more often than not, in between their masters' feet, no man falling, though, and the dogs, despite their masters' kicks, still keeping up, with their tongues out and their tails high, as if Missy Janie were something that had been caught and was about to be cooked, and they, the dogs, were going to be given the scraps after the hunters had finished with her, the dogs pawing, sucking at her bones in the dirt, carrying her bones off to some low dog-dug ditch which could be easily found whenever the dogs needed another mouthful-mmm-taste of Missy Janie.

Walking slowly, out in front of the hunters and their dogs, leading them back into town, was Pastor Whisser, wearing his cape, the one with the hood that he wears to welcome the new into chapel and to bury the dead in the surrounding hills, on top of which you can look down into the valley to see all of town, a small edge of a place you cannot believe you are from, the Pastor walking with the slow-upping dirt-drag of his shoes, his hands pushed palm-flat together, held just out from his lips, praying lips of "Our Father, our protecting Father, be you the saviour we know you to be, and grant us your glory peace, lead us into your mercy singing," the Pastor praying this over and over, stopping often to touch those near to him who seemed to want to be touched, those reaching out to him, the townswomen with their babies mostly, although nearly everyone had come out to watch, except for Dora and the other wives of the pastors, who were stuck inside chapel, baking the meal they made each week to take over to the black orphans, who lived quite a truck ride away, in the northernmost part of the county. As the Pastor prayed on, he knelt, chinning his face toward the dirt, asking us that we do the same, our mouths in each other's hair, so close and so many were we, only Missy Janie left high on the shoulders of the hunters, who were not kneeling, but in full-out-to-the-knee squats, Missy Janie above us as some sort of angel as we were all in a moment with ourselves, lifting our hearts to the Lord God Almighty and giving Him our thanks and praise.

The Pastor raised himself from out of the dirt, the towns-women kneeling near to him, leaning forward, down onto their stomachs, they dusting off the knees of the Pastor's pants as he crossed over us, "In the name of the Father and of the Son, and of the Holy Spirit. Amen. Amen. Amen. Amen. Amen."

Jesus.

The kids got out of this, those who took to the trees, that is, to have the best look of Missy Janie that could be had of her from far away and with so many people, and I, too, wanting to be so up there with them, looking down at her, seeing her wet-stiffed up to her clothing—her hair, nips, everything I had touched pushing erect-through, I was sure. I stayed on the ground, stayed with my age, you know, too scared I was that Jan, my name for her, would no longer look as good to me. No, really, I thought she would look better to me than she had when we had been together on the shore.

When the Pastor, hunters, and dogs had moved on far enough for the crowd to circle in around to follow to Dr. Samuels's place, his place past the few stores we do have in town, near the chapel and the school, I heard one of the kids say, "Her teeth must still be in the river."

"And her hair," another said, and the kids dropped from out of the trees, some of the younger ones sliding right off the limbs onto the backs of the bigger ones, some lifted over one shoulder to be carried sack-of-potato style, some falling into the dirt as they ran so hard to keep up, running for who could find the best and most of what was left of Missy Janie in the river.

Not much of her was there to be found. Not enough to make you think that anything, least of all something like her, had happened that day. Some blood in water and on grass, which could easily have been explained away as animal blood, since the dogs do bring down to the water whatever half-live, dripping-blood rabbit, bird, or squirrel they have caught with their mouths, and since the kids are known to wade through the green-dirt water, heavy stones in hand, to brain the lizards which have come out onto the rocks to sun themselves, lizards slit open on the shore and left there to dry by the kids, who go on to hunt for more lizards, as many as are needed—lots —to make the bands that the kids wear around their ankles and their wrists. Or should I say wore? For the lizard bands were soon replaced by the ones I watched the kids collect for, bands of Missy Janie hair and grass with her blood, for which Pastor Whisser whomped the kids several good cuffs, me watching his hand spread on their faces as the kids walked back to their families, me fearing for what he would do to me if he ever found out that I wore way down on the long-looping bottom of my chain no Jesus Christ cross any longer but a finger-length worth of hair cut from the back underside of Missy Janie's head. Her idea, it was, for us to wear each other's hair, since we never could wear rings, locket hearts, or anything else like that, which would have shown everybody in town how we felt for one another and would have probably ended up getting us stoned out of our town, the next town over, and the town after that, too. That is how fast the paper spreads word about our county; us last seen running in Fordly, the paper would read, with a trophy feast of fox on our heads for the hunter who could nail us before we crossed the state line, and shot we would be, faith in our hunters I have, and then drug back along the ground into town, the way they did to that man who burnt schoolman Fletcher's home years back, our skin, like that man's, rubbed off our faces and arms, pebble-filled and dirtied with blood, we hardly recognizable anymore, not even to our own mothers, and burnt to a smoking ash outside of chapel, where the poles had been shoved, we no God children being sent back to the Devil our maker.

Never would happen, though, for my hair found roped-tied to the bottom of Missy Janie's chain was taken by Dr. Samuels and Pastor Whisser to be more of the same hair that had been growing between her breasts, devil hair that she had pulled out of her and kept on a chain waiting for the spell the Devil would have her do, a spell which would have given him way into all our souls, had not the hair, this hair, held right here in the Pastor's hand, been taken out of her, this child of the Lord, now seated before us on the altar, where once she had stood playing the holy bells of Christmas, she now saved as we all were saved from the death of the Devil to live in the mighty light of the Lord God Our Father.

That girl looked none too saved to me. Despite the blue-clam calm of her face, her body was twisted in upon itself, slumped-limp in its sitting to one side of the chair Dr. Samuels drove all the night for to fetch from up city, her sitting as if some other person were sitting in the chair with her, that other person taking up so much of the seat that Missy Janie had to squeeze herself to that one side, her one shoulder hiked high as if resting on the other person's shoulder, her one arm crossed over to lay upon the other tied to the armrest, her legs, the legs of a child now, crossed so tight her feet were almost on top of one another, and her head arching in a back-tilting, slow-spray scan of the chapel ceiling, as if there were some-thing new to be seen up there, something which only she could see, that made her make that sound, that low-wheeze-high-purr kind of sound that made the bells call and the dogs paw at the chapel doors.

That girl, I tried to tell myself, was none no girl of mine, but of course, how kid of me, of course she was, she was still my Jan. I was ashamed of myself for being ashamed of that girl, being afraid of her, she just a girl after all, and me afraid to touch her, to have her breathe on me, for what if, what if somehow by swallowing her breath I were to end up as she, all mind in a body locked dead-alive. When I saw Pastor Whisser touch her as he spoke on his holy words, smoothing his hands along her cheeks, over her ears, and into her hair, her head stopping in its arching scan to lay back silent in his hands, when I saw that, I pushed on through the knees of those who were sitting next to me, ran up onto the altar, and before they could stop me, I grabbed the white robe of a dress they had put her in and pulled her onto me, she as light as a child in my arms, her breasts pushing into my face and me hearing that sound of hers as I kissed her for all to see—what to care—me so in there again with my Jan. I think she must have felt inside of me, too, for as Pastor Whisser reached his hands in to take her off of me, there came from out of her a cry for which I was blamed, a cry that sounded to me to be that of her body trying to twist itself free, and as I moved to follow, someone reached his hands underneath my arms and up past my shoulders to lock his hands flat on top of my head, me kept back by this prisoner-check-for-the-gun hold, I think only the hunters know, this hunter saying "Quiet" in my ear, "Easy, girl, it's all right, come on, girl, let's just be easy now," as I watched Pastor Whisser carry Missy Janie, her head in his throat and her legs limp over his arms, as if he were carrying her to the altar of their wedding, Pastor Whisser lifting her down into the chair, in which she stays now, but for the baths the wives of the pastors take turns giving her, me allowed to dry and powder and nightgown Missy Janie whenever Dora takes her turn at bathing the cripple, her skin feeling to me the way her skin used to feel, water-wet as skin that can feel, me lifting her hand to touch me as I touch down on her, her face not changing, and sometimes I am in the bed beside her, me on the blanket I wrap over her when I am through, the best times I have with Missy Janie no longer happening but for in my mind alone.

Most days, we in town keep Missy Janie outside, walking her all through town and taking her, when Dr. Samuels does not need his truck, towns over to walk her over there, the

whole county probably knowing about her by now, due more
to the paper than to the few trips we have taken her on. When
it comes to be my day with Missy Janie, I push her to the bridge
way up over the Moosha River, and she gets that look, which
Pastor Whisser says is the look of God content on her face, me
taking her as near as is safe for her to be where the kids are
screaming for whoever has just jumped, and leaving her to
some other kid, one of the bigger ones, who seem not to mind
much, I go to stand on the edge of the bridge, look back at her
from out of my hips, to see her as a dream-of-a-girl feeling, the
girl that she used to be, the one with the two-fingers-in-the-
mouth whistle that kept her body from breaking in the cedar
burst of water, and there I go—watch me, watch me—I again
am reaching for the rope. Q

Winter

I once saw a film in which girls in black dresses danced in a courtyard while a woman looked on. The girls danced in rings around younger girls, who sat on the ground with their legs turned out like the spokes of a wheel the girls were dancing around. In the center of the courtyard, which seemed to me to be the courtyard of a school, the woman stood and watched the girls, moving very little, her eyes flitting to the camera. At the end of this, the film slows down, little by little, until the hands of the girls freeze in a blur and their skirts stand still in midair. Then the film ends.

I saw this film in winter.

Later, I became a teacher at a school for children who showed promise. The film came back to me in my memory then, always in winter, perhaps because the girls in the courtyard looked cold. The film was black and white, broken in places, and not well repaired, and for some reason there was no music for the girls to dance to.

I am not a teacher now. I have given up teaching. I think that I will work in a museum, or perhaps a library. I have experience. There are many people I know here in London, but I no longer know them. I walk through the city on Saturdays, to places I have never seen before. For my fortieth birthday, I intend to redecorate my apartment, so that I can stay at home more and work. I am trying to write a little book about Cézanne.

It is difficult to write, because I am easily distracted. Perhaps being distracted has something to do with turning forty. When I am working, things I have seen at another time, things I have done, occur to me.

This, for instance. I am standing on the edge of a boat in

Derwentwater. It is raining. I am standing there for only a moment or two, but the rain lasts all afternoon. A girl in a yellow raincoat slips on the dock and a man helps her up. Then they come aboard the boat and sit down.

I'm there for my vacation. I am still teaching. My sister has come with me, and although it is only the third day, I have told her that I am going back to London. I no longer need a vacation, I said.

But I'm not going back. I am going to Scotland after my sister gets on the train. I want to be alone now. If my sister knew this, she would not understand it.

She is thirty-one years old. As we cross the lake, the mist hangs down to the water like fog and my sister is sitting with her hands in her pockets. From my perch on the boat, I see a girl, coatless, standing on the dock. A black car drives up and the girl gets inside. It seems graceful to me, as does everything on the lake.

At the far end of the dock, a child is lifted to the shoulders of a man in a red coat. She is held there while the man walks.

I was teaching school for the fifth year and would catch pneumonia before I returned to London, before I left the boat, before my sister boarded the train. I was twenty-nine years old. As I said, there are people in London who know me. Once I stopped teaching, I no longer saw Marie Geronet. She was a teacher at the same school, a teacher of history. We used to walk home together and talk about the students, who seemed to take all our energy. Marie Geronet had a lover at the time. The man invested all his savings in a clothing factory in Taiwan. Marie refused to talk to the man about it, because she thought it was immoral to invest in such a business. The man was black, a very slight man with a history of bad investments. Perhaps Marie Geronet and her lover are still lovers. The factory closed down a year later and the fellow lost all his savings.

Another woman, Clara Sur, lived in my building for a

while. Then she moved to the outskirts of the city. She would have more space there, she said. When she lived in my building, we drank coffee together in her apartment, which was larger than mine and completely white. When Clara Sur went out in the evenings, she wore enormous black capes that made her look as if she were going to be photographed. When she moved to the outskirts, I never saw her anymore, except at a play once, months later, where she showed me the dirt under her fingernails.

Signs of her garden, she said.

She said she was writing to a man from South America who was a revolutionary and would not be back in the country for several years, if ever. She said she felt great freedom in that.

It isn't that I have no lovers of my own. There is a man in Kintbury who would like me to leave London for him. I have known him for a long time. He is much older than I am—I was twenty-three when I met him. He was forty.

He had hired me to do his typing. I had not yet started teaching and I saw his notice at the post office in Kintbury when I was visiting a friend. "Typist wanted," the notice said, "to type large manuscript. Must be fast and accurate and not mind explicit passages. Excellent pay."

He was an American, a retired man with lots of money.

I corrected his work, changed sentences, incidents. His name was Park, or did I mention this? Park Wallace.

It was nearly six months later, after the trip to Scotland and my first years of teaching, that I saw Park Wallace again. I was very depressed at that time and I had broken things in my apartment. It was Clara Sur who let him in, and who found me with the furniture overturned and the windows open, rain coming in, my dishes on the floor. I was sorting them by shape. I explained to Park Wallace that I had pushed myself to the limits. I was glad to see him.

As I am putting my sister on the train, she asks me to send a wire to her husband. "Tell him to be there early," my sister says. "I hate to wait in the dark."

The wind lifts the scattered papers from the tracks and twirls them briefly in the air. I promise to send the telegram. My sister's hair has got itself gray, is pulled back from her face in a braid. She was the only one of us who married. Even on vacations, she would stand apart, looking at something—the horizon, birds.

In Edinburgh, I met a girl with black eyeliner in wide strokes around her eyes. She said she was lost. She said her group was somewhere inside the castle on a tour, so she was smoking a cigarette in the park and thinking about a taxi. I sat down to watch the pigeons, which flew from place to place.

The girl said, "I've got to get out of here. This place makes me crazy."

"Why?" I said.

"The tourists," the girl said.

In my flat last week, I was looking for photographs of trips. I had just talked to Park Wallace on the telephone. He said he was coming up to talk to me, and I told him I did not have time for talk.

The photographs were of me with my sister. One was missing, the one of me standing on a rock. It is about to rain, and I am looking at the shore. The castle is behind me.

When Park Wallace comes up to my place, he says that he wants me to leave London with him. But why don't we go eat something first? he says.

In the cab, I tell Park Wallace that I want to see a movie. We look out the window at the rain. We ride around for a long time, looking for a theater. **Q**

Houses on the Avenues

People think that mentally retarded people laugh at stupid things. It's not true. When there is something on television and everyone from the canned laughter starts laughing, Rusty turns around in the chair where he sits close to the television set, and he looks at us, to make sure we are all laughing, before he starts to laugh.

My mother is not old, but I can see that her legs are starting to look old. I think about my mother, and I wonder what my mother would do if she had a day to herself when she did not have to work at the rest home or take care of Rusty. I can see my mother walking along the sidewalk, in the silver coat that my mother used to wear when she was married to my father. I imagine my mother walking through town and out onto the avenues, and I can see her looking at the houses that she passes, houses on the avenues with verandas that themselves look out onto the water.

My boyfriend and I take Rusty to the zoo, and Rusty runs ahead of us to see the birds. We all stand looking at the birds, and then we walk back to the gate and we look at the animals with everyone else.

Sometimes my mother comes into the bathroom, where I am getting ready for the zoo, and she talks to me.

"You think Rusty knows what day it is?" my mother says. "Rusty don't know if it's Tuesday or if it's Wednesday or if it's Saturday," my mother says.

On the way home from the zoo, we stop at Big Boy for hamburgers, which we take home to eat with my mother. My mother is still wearing her uniform, and we all watch Lawrence Welk. Rusty sits in his regular chair, close to the television, and he watches to see if we are laughing. Sometimes Rusty laughs with us and sometimes he does not. When Rusty doesn't laugh, I know it is because he is remembering the Sunday when we had dinner at my boyfriend Greg's parents'.

Greg's mother invited my family to dinner, and I could tell that my mother was nervous, because she kept wiping at her mouth with her handkerchief. When my mother is nervous, she makes Rusty nervous. Rusty was sitting in the living room on the couch when I came out of my bedroom. He had his hands folded in his lap and he would not talk to me. Rusty was wearing his blue suit, and from the side you could not tell that Rusty was retarded, with his wide shoulders and his thick blond hair.

Mr. Martin opened the door when we got to the Martins', and he took our coats. We sat down in the living room, and Mrs. Martin brought us cups of hot cider. Rusty sat on the ottoman in front of the TV, and he balanced the cup and saucer on his lap. Mrs. Martin sat next to my mother, and she asked my mother what it was like to work in a rest home.

"It's all right except for the bedpans," my mother said.

Mrs. Martin got up from the couch and went into the kitchen. Then it was time for us to eat dinner, and everyone moved into the dining room. We sat at the Martins' dining-room table, where Mrs. Martin had ham and scalloped potatoes sitting on the table in fancy dishes, and an orange Jell-O salad. I could see that Rusty was still nervous, because he kept sweating and wiping his face with his napkin. I was afraid he would spill something, even though Rusty never spills things.

Mrs. Martin asked my mother about the things my mother liked to do when she was not working, and my mother answered her questions. Then Mrs. Martin turned to Rusty. "What do you study at your school?" Mrs. Martin said.

"We learn about taking buses," Rusty said.

Mrs. Martin made a small sound, and then she reached for her iced tea, and she spilled it onto the white lace tablecloth. Rusty started laughing, and he kept laughing even when my mother told him to stop. Mrs. Martin started to laugh, and then she cried and left the table.

No one could think of what to say to Mr. Martin, so we kept eating Mrs. Martin's ham and potatoes, and then the Jell-O.

After dinner, we sat in the living room again. Mrs. Martin came and passed out little dinner mints, and Mr. Martin brought us cups of coffee. We watched a special on TV, and Rusty sat on the ottoman. When someone on television said something funny, Rusty turned to see if we were laughing, but he himself did not laugh.

We drove home and my mother went right to bed. Then Rusty went to bed. I stayed up, thinking about Mrs. Martin and about my mother. I thought that Mrs. Martin was probably lying next to Mr. Martin and that she would be thinking that Greg and I would have a baby like Rusty.

I thought about my mother, and I could see my mother walking along in her silver coat, looking at the houses on the avenues, the ones that had the verandas. I think that my mother would have a package of crackers inside her coat and that my mother would feed some of the crackers to the geese before she herself walked out into the water. **Q**

Cousins

When I was five and she seven, she took me up to her room, closed the door to a crack, and let me stick my finger inside her. The daffodils of her walls danced on black stems. Across the hall, her mother watched a game show. It felt like nothing new—it felt like wet sand.

"Wet sand?" she breathed against my ear. "It's me."

We went outside to our shared driveway and threw a softball back and forth over a low telephone wire. I could never catch it. It came down from its arc like a balloon and then exploded like a rock in my hands. At dinner, on a picnic table between her home and mine, her father, my uncle, waved me over with a promise—"I have something for you." He slid the glasses from my nose. "Watch," he said, and began to smear my glasses with peanut butter. My mother, her spring skirt a fountain to her shins, snatched the eyeglasses back from my uncle, saying, "Carl, don't tease the boy." She pulled me into our garage and brought the door down, held me in the light of my father's extension lamp, and said, "Be still." Then she tugged my shorts to my ankles and on the whiteness of my thigh found a raised mole, which she pinched until a stick of orange pus poked out and fell into the folds of her skirt.

"There," she said, and I did not touch my cousin again. **Q**

Counting

Uncle Woody's dad died, and he left camp and never came back. Some other uncle took us over, taught us the things we were supposed to learn about regulators and cleaning our masks and the bends, and gave us our badges at the farewell dinner.

Mr. Ricklin's dad died, and he left school for four days, during which time Mrs. Walstrom had the entire fifth grade every day, all day, and we saw movies about the Civil War and played inside games at recess, because it rained without relief. We played sockey, kicking a rolled-up sock between two goals on a hardwood floor in our bare feet. When Mr. Ricklin came back, he sometimes stopped in the middle of a lesson and said nothing at all, and we said nothing, either. Then, gradually, almost so we couldn't see it, Mr. Ricklin resumed being himself, and even though this was his only year at our school, we stopped remembering him as ever being any way else.

Dwayne's dad died, and although Dwayne had left our school the year before and his father did not make even a shadow on my memory—whether he was tall or short, fat or thin—I tried to go see Dwayne. I walked down a lot of streets smelling of grass and gardens and turned corners to places I hadn't been since a long time before, and I felt important and sad and wise, because I was going to tell Dwayne how sorry I was that his dad had died. But when I got to Dwayne's, there were cars parked in the driveway and on both sides of the street and the front door was shut and in the windows I could see many people. I just turned back the way I had come and told myself I would find Dwayne some other time, to tell him how sorry I was.

My mom's dad died, and I knew it had happened because they were all up in the hallway, turning on and off lights and shuffling from clothes, and it was just as the night was fading, and I understood that they had already left me and come back and were going to bed, because he had died and there would be no more worrying. I slid out of bed and walked down the hall to their room, where my dad was in the bathroom shaving with an electric razor, and on the bed my mother lay curled in a heap. I got into the bed and lay down beside her, and I said, "Did he?"

Nigel's father died, and I felt terrible for him. We posted an emergency meeting for the dormitory and then I trooped over to his apartment, wondering what I was going to say and how I was going to say it. I said, "Nigel, I'm very sorry about your father," and Nigel grinned with his crowded greenish teeth and looked away and excused himself to go to the bathroom.

Jim's father passed away, and very few of us in the office could bring ourselves to say anything. The truth was, he'd been passing away for years and we were beginning to doubt whether he had ever existed. So Jim's father died and we didn't send Jim cards or flowers or even give him extra smiles at work.

Then the medical people around my dad all turned to stare at me, their pens and instruments touching air, as if waiting for my answers, which I as yet did not know. **Q**

Between Stations

Walking home, he always counted the number of steps from the station, no matter which station he happened to be coming from. His house was midway between two stations, or as close to midway as he could calculate without actually measuring, and so he could get off at either station. Even if his house were not midway, it would not have made a difference to him. He liked having the choice. He did not want to become paralyzed by habit. By getting off at the near station one night, the far another night, he could add an element of uncertainty to his life. Riding the train from work, he would deliberately postpone the decision until the last instant. In this way, his commute was filled with excitement, a certain tension.

He realized that he was wasting time on those evenings when he got off at the far station. But as long as he was in no hurry, he liked to ride past his house. Looking down from the embankment, he could see it plainly. With its turrets and dormers and gables, it was too large to miss. On blue winter evenings, he could see the house silhouetted against the dark sky, the lights warm and comforting, white smoke trailing from the chimney. Or in the summer twilight, across the radiant lawns and gardens, he would often see his wife, waiting on the porch or working in the yard.

The train went by so rapidly that all he usually had was a flickering glimpse of the house. But that was enough. His imagination, his memory, filled in the details, and there were times he could swear he saw small children playing on the steps or in the yard, as if the train window had opened onto the past. And on certain nights, the light was such that the house, rather than the train, seemed to be moving, hurtling by. It was a relief when the train stopped and he could get off, put his feet to earth again and be reassured that his house was in the same place it had been the night before, that it would be the night after, that he could close his eyes and count the number of steps, from either station, and end up at his own front porch.

That was what was so disorienting about the chair, that summer evening he arrived home and found it missing. He quickly sensed it was not in its usual place on the porch. His first thought was that it had been stolen. It was an old chair, sturdy and probably made by hand, and for all he knew, it could have been an antique. He was never particularly fond of it himself. It was uncomfortable and he rarely sat in it. But it was nothing like the flimsy chairs they made today, which was why it was irreplaceable and a likely target for thieves. Standing there on the porch in the fading light, he was gripped by an inexplicable sadness, almost as strong as grief.

His wife was in the kitchen, cutting up something for dinner. "The wicker chair is gone," he said. "From the front porch." He brushed past her and stood at the refrigerator. "The chair is gone," he said. "Did you call the police?"

"Why would I call the police?" she said.

"About the chair," he said. "It's gone."

She looked at him without expression. "It's been gone for a long time," she said.

He knew nothing of the kind, and started to tell her so, but what was the use of telling her what she already knew as well as he did? He refused to let himself be drawn into her nonsense and resolved to say no more about it, to forget about it. But he woke during the night, remembering, and quietly got out of bed so that he could go downstairs and reassure himself that the chair really was missing.

He was waking up almost every night now, wondering about the chair, and as he searched the house for it, he seemed to find more rooms than he thought his house had, most of them as filled with cobwebs as a crypt, the curtains stiff and gray with dust, the rugs worn bare. It looked as if his wife had not entered them in years, much less given them the cleaning they badly needed. If he had not been operating in such secrecy, he would have mentioned this neglect to her. But as it was, he moved through the house very quietly, not wanting to raise any dust, for fear that he would sneeze.

The wicker chair was nowhere in the house, though, and its absence maddened him. It made him sick to ride the train home. Watching the landscape go by, he thought he saw none of the buildings, streets, or parks that usually marked his return.

One night, everything looked so unfamiliar that he panicked, afraid that he'd missed his stations. He ran to the door, reached up, and pulled the red handle on the emergency cord. There was a mighty jolt. He managed to hold on to the cord and pull it again. The train bucked ahead, then shuddered to a stop.

He could hear shouts, shrieks of alarm from the other cars. The doors opened and he leaped out. He landed off balance, one foot slipped in the gravel, and he slid partway down the embankment, tearing a pant leg and scraping his knee. He struggled to his feet and limped through the dense brush to a chain-link fence, found a spot where he could get through, and slid under on his back.

He did not know where he was, only that he had come out into an alley, somewhere between stations. He followed the alley to the street. But it was one he did not recognize. He thought he might still be stunned by the leap from the train. The streets were empty. The houses looked as if they had been abandoned.

He walked along the street that paralleled the tracks, knowing that he would eventually reach the station. Once he got there, he could always find his way home. The air was as cold and gray as iron, the sidewalk slick with soggy patches of fallen leaves. He felt a brisk wind at his neck and pulled his collar against it. He remembered his wife telling him not to hunch his shoulders, but what else could he do? He had not expected it to turn so cold.

He was greatly relieved when he came to the station. There was no mistake. From half a block away, he could make out its bulky ramparts, its I-beam pillars, painted an odious pale blue. He was approaching the station from the wrong direction—opposite the one he always took—which accounted for his feeling of dislocation. But he knew he could close his eyes now and still find the way to his front door.

Coming to a corner, he turned down a street in the direction of his home, then immediately realized that he had made a wrong turn. This was not his street at all. The houses were different—of a different style and vintage.

He knew exactly what he had done, if not quite how he had done it. In his haste to get home, he had not paid careful attention to where he was going, and in the process he had strayed slightly off course. He shuffled ahead, knowing that he could detour onto his own street at the next intersection. But when he reached the intersection, he did not know which direction to go, and so he struck out instinctively and, as it turned out, blindly. Nothing looked right. It all looked wrong.

If he could just get back to the station, either station, he assured himself, he could make it home without any trouble. He could do it with his eyes closed. But in crossing streets, weaving through alleys and the like, he had taken such an erratic and circuitous path, made so many turns and shortcuts, that he had lost all sense of direction. The overcast sky was no help. Whichever way he went seemed to take him farther from home. He stood on the corner for a while, listening for the rumble of a train, hoping that it would lead him back to the station. But all he heard was the sound of crows, the wind, distant sirens.

He thought about knocking on a door, asking for help. But he decided the best thing to do, the only thing to do, was to stay in one place. He sat down. He drew in his legs and hugged his knees for warmth. He was waiting for his wife to come and take him home. **Q**

Vaporware

So I sell vaporware for a living, what's that prove? The money's decent, and maybe the stuff'll work the way the company hopes, the way I guarantee my customers. You can't hang me for giving it a shot. This is America, last I heard.

A woman leaves messages on my machine. She insists she still loves me, uses words like "anodyne" and "inevitable"— but then why'd she move 751 miles away with my brother? I answer the messages. My phone bill is enormous. I wrote a postcard saying this is ridiculous. On the other side were *Greetings from Colorado* and a jackalope the size of a bull. She gave it to me years ago, during a "cute" period. "Cute" was *her* word. I trust "cute" about as far as I can spit an eight ball.

So here I sit, naked, taking a day off from peddling vaporware. I drank coffee till noon, beer after that, watched two Steve Martin movies on the VCR, and read half an inch of *The Executioner's Song.* I'd bet the farm that postcard arrived today; she'll plan to give herself time to think it over but won't make it past sundown. I debate whether to put in *The Jerk.* The phone rings. The machine answers.

"You return my present to tell me I'm not worth a few toll calls? I'm not that easy to erase. I love you and don't you forget it. This is the eighties, lover. This is America, last I heard." **Q**

Just Name Someplace

I received a birthday card today from my first husband. Inside, it says that the most interesting thing I could do with my life would be to end it. Now, where would he get a card like that, what kind of shop? I wonder what other kinds of cards a place like that might have.

My birthday was today. What I wished for from Daddy I didn't get. I wished for a pine-box coffin and a plot as far away from home as he could possibly find. It could be in a respectable cemetery in another city. I don't mind. Just not in the city in which we live.

Daddy gave me another horse. He says it is a fine mare with all the proper papers. Later, Daddy is sending a picture of it the photographer is taking. It will say *Happy Birthday, Myna. Love, Daddy* in the bottom corner.

We all know where we will be buried—up on the hill behind the house. Granddaddy started us being buried there again after a skip in history. Granddaddy used to walk around Sissy's room at night when she was little. She used to think it was because no one looked out after his grave. Darnell used to run the bush hog around the cemetery fence, but he would leave the tombstones untended. You know how those people are. The help.

Sissy used to cry in the night about Granddaddy's visits. She used to come and get in my bed after Momma and Daddy kicked her out of theirs. In the mornings, you could look out the Florida room and see Sissy up on the hill, bent over with a bucket and a brush. Scrubbing.

My first husband dresses the dead for a living. Just like his father and his father before. In high school, he used to take me into the funeral parlor. It's the only one in town. He would show me the workroom, and then we'd make out in the chapel.

Once, I brought him off with my hand while he was lying in a box. We had along paper towels with us from the workroom. We didn't want him to spot the satin.

My husband and I never did it before we were married. We had plenty of chances. We used to go on top of the hill at night. You could see anyone leave the house across the pasture. I would be worked up across the cool marble. Do it, I would say —do it, put it in. But he would keep looking down toward the house, where the lights were on and Momma and Daddy and Sissy were watching television in the Florida room. They're all still down there, do it, I'd say. I can't, he'd say, and I'd button up my windbreaker. On the way back, he'd make me bring him off with my hands along the pasture fence. Sometimes, the horses would come over. They were thinking we were leaving them something to eat.

After we were married, it was all right. He had the house where we lived next to his work. I had the money. I never went next door after we were married. He washed well before dinner. His hands were always soft from the scrub and smelled like gardenias. His fingers were short and warm, his nails neat and the cuticles trimmed. He had to hold so many hands.

We knew everyone he buried. I was often among the friends of the family. My husband stood near the cars. Later, he would say, You should have seen the nubber on Mr. Tate, or on Daty Smithwicke the additional nipples. After we were married, he never let me in the workroom, so I never knew these secrets until after the earth had taken them back.

Those nights it was all right. I made him put his fingers in me everywhere until it hurt. I wanted the smell of everything over that smell of flowers.

One night, the deputy brought a white male in a brown sport coat around to the door in back. The deputy pulled back a piece of canvas. I was in the bedroom window, looking down. The white male was missing most of his face. He was a man of any color in that light.

My husband said the deputy needed a drink. It was after

midnight. They put whiskey in their coffee. At four o'clock, the doorbell rang. My husband went down in his robe. The white male in the brown sport coat was sitting on our porch. The deputy said it must have been some kids. He said the man was cold when he brought him in. He said, You saw him, to my husband. Sure, my husband said.

I wanted us to move. I told my husband I wanted him to talk to Daddy. Daddy could get him a job at the racetrack. He wouldn't have to work with dead bodies. I said I was tired of being married to an undertaker, and he hit me.

I went to see a doctor. The doctor said to find something to interest me, to find a hobby. There is nothing I can make that I can't just buy and like better. No one can understand that.

I tried a different way with my husband. I said he could retire and we could travel on my money. Anywhere he wanted to go. Name it. Could he just name someplace, please?

My husband spent more time next door.

Night after night.

You would have thought our town had had a plague or something, the amount of time he spent over there. I wondered if things went on. In high school once, he brought me some intestine in a jar.

Some mornings I would wake up just so I could lie at the top of the stairs and think. I didn't clean house. I didn't clean myself. I liked the smell of life.

Have you ever heard of morticians coming home and making their wives take cold baths and then making them lie real still in bed while they do it to them? Have you?

I was frightened by the sound of the doorbell. No one came to visit. Momma and Daddy didn't. They said I had married the mortician. They barely came to the service. We had it in the chapel next door. Not many people came.

I began imagining him getting an infection next door. I hoped his hearse would have an accident and the coffin would slide up from behind and crush him against the wheel. One night he caught me sawing his seat belts with a steak knife. What, Myna? he said.

I know things were going on next door. He won't admit it. A man has to have something. No one came and no one went, except the stiffs in and out through the back. I know. Sometimes, I would watch the place next door all day in my nightgown from the window.

I carried a steak knife in my robe. I almost stabbed Sissy with it when she rang the doorbell. She had been to China. What's the matter? I said. She said, You have a smell.

I went to live with Sissy and her cats. We all sleep together in Sissy's big bed. Cats are my hobby. We hunt mice in Sissy's fields out back. They are part of Daddy's fields, too. Momma and Daddy got my money back from my husband. People in our town are still dying, so I have to see him sometimes at funerals. He tries to take my hand, but I won't let him. He smiles and winks like he knows my secrets already. I won't have any of it.

I don't think about the time I lived with him next door to his work. Tonight, I'll hold Sissy close and I won't think about him at all. Imagine him sending me this birthday card on my birthday. His warm hands on my cold dead body?

I won't have it.

I just will not. **Q**

Spoils; or, The Sea of Ten Thousand Sciences

[1]

It was like clots of milk floating up in water—the way all of the fingernails of the whip girl looked. They also looked to me to be each of them trimmed down close to those places on each of the ends of her fingers where the fingernails of the whip girl rooted her finger-end skin. The whip girl trimmed all of them that way but the one of them which was the nail on the one finger of hers that she left long and that she filed to a point and that she lacquered to be hard, almost as if the whip girl wanted to use that one fingernail in particular of hers to open up a letter.

I saw why it was that her fingernails were milk-dotted and why it was that she cut her fingernails short enough for her to fist-ball her fingers as both being because of the same reason. I put it all down to what the whip girl told me she had done —despoiling the bodies of the cousin-killers whom the whip girl told me she had left down on their backs, knocked there by the lash of her steel whip.

I found out, in the case of the pigtail girl, that the pigtail girl was also someone's cousin. When I actually got to see the cousin of the pigtail girl—at the same time me getting to see truly how tall the cousin of the pigtail girl was—I could not figure how that cousin had grown so, when, all along, the pigtail girl herself looked as if she was from a mother and a father that wanted to keep everything they made shorter than they were. When I looked at the pigtail girl, I imagined how she might not even be tall enough to lift her chest over the tray for putting chalk in at the bottom of the blackboard. I also imagined that all of the pigtail girl could weigh no more than my leg or my shoulder, because, when I looked at her, that was how small the pigtail girl looked.

But then there was one time when I looked at her when the pigtail girl sat down and painted her fingernails Double Joy red and came over to me, shaking a finger at me, and I was watching that swinging stoplight shine on that fingernail of that finger of hers.

"My cousin going to get a gun and come fuck your shit up," the pigtail girl stared at me and said.

There was a boy who called me Gregor.

Someone sat in the seat that was the one between my seat and the seat that the boy who called me Gregor sat in. The boy who called me Gregor carried a big head on top of his shoulders, which were close together and which did not go far, it looked to me like, toward putting any kind of a space between the bony front of his chest and the hard braid of his spine. His head was really something, though—like a blow from a hammer might not be enough to break it; I think that, to the boy who called me Gregor, his head was just a thing that he could use to make sure that his ways to make brushstrokes stayed safe up in there in his head, or maybe written out in there, all of those ways of his for writing written out, on the inside of the boy who called me Gregor's brain.

The boy who called me Gregor mostly sat and used his brush over there, a seat and a person away from me. Once in a while, though, the boy would make his neck longer and at the same time turn his head so that, with his eyes in that big-looking head, he would be looking around the person sitting between us, looking at me. When the boy looked over at me like that, he would ask me what I was doing over where I was, sitting in that seat of mine. There were also times when I wanted him to tell me the answer to things, and that was when the boy who called me Gregor would jump out of his seat over to where I was in my seat and would put his face on my arm so that I could feel the breath that he breathed out breathed on my arm.

"Gregor," the boy once whispered, "starting now, one time each week, my father will meet a truck, to get melon for me to sell—twenty-five cent apiece for the melons, Gregor."

The boy who called me Gregor once said to me that his mother and his father had brought him all the way over the ocean over to here, all of the way from the pirate coast in the south of the place that was the place that the boy's mother had given birth to him in, which was also the same place that she, herself, the boy said, was once given birth to in. But beyond telling me where it was that his mother and his father came from, the boy who called me Gregor did not tell me another thing about these people.

If you ask me, the boy who called me Gregor did not want to talk about his mother and his father. That boy only wanted to tell me about the place that all three of them had come out of their mothers in.

For one thing, the boy wanted me to know the way the place would sound each spring to me when the people there all took cooking pots and cooking buckets and cooking ladles and cooking tubs and filled them all up to the brimming point with water and then threw all of the water all one on another, all of them there on the pirate coast—all of the people there getting all wet all at once.

The whip girl had her long sharp one in the corner of her mouth, pressing on her lip, turning her lip out, letting me see the inside of her while she told me about the events that had happened to her and about the events that had happened, as far as she knew, to her uncle, who, the whip girl said, had been the one who had taught her to steel-whip, so that she would be safe after coming over here to this place.

"My cousin, when he got here," the girl said, "some peo-ple came after him who were not from a group. So when I got here, I went after them and I took their pants down. I left some marks on them," she said, "I did."

The whip girl showed me the keys and the socks of those people whom she had whipped—which were the things that had belonged to those people that she had kept for herself. There was a panda key ring. There were socks, which were thin and blue-colored and which had bright pink pinstripes. The whip girl moved the hand of hers that had the one finger with the one long one on it through the spoils as if the spoils were the water and she was stirring a bath.

"If you can't handle him by yourself—if you want me to tell my other cousin, then I could," she said. "Then he could tell him for your sake that his head will blow up," she said.

"Fuck off," the pigtail girl cooed at us.

[2]

I crossed the ocean back with the sun, and walked around in the city that the whip girl had grown up in. The city had a place called the Upper Corner and a place called the Lower Corner.

I walked through the breadth of it—both the corners and the suburbs—the whole of the whole city. One end of the place was the place that was the beginning of my walk, and the opposite other end was the place that was the end of my walk, the situs where I went to sleep on the road. I began walking just before the sun went down, and I did not get to the end of my walk until I could see the sun again. When I was where I was when I was done, my legs were the way they feel when you put pins in to heal them and twist. That was why I walked through half that city walking bent over as if I was looking for a key that I might have dropped on the road.

On my way through the corners, I saw them sleeping in chairs, sitting in the streets. Some of them sat on stools which looked to me like dog-big bamboo spiders.

I believe I had chosen the sitters who were women to ask

where I was because I kept thinking of a steel-whipping uncle in each of the men. I remember I walked up behind two of them who were two old women sitting on stools.

"Aunties!" I growled.

Then, later, a sitter grabbed my hand.

"Nephew," she said, "speak English."

[3]

Rainbow Mouth Park, the whip girl said, was the place in the city where she had lived with her uncle.

"My cousin is very arrogant. He is beset with mischief. He would come to my uncle's house in the park and drink all the soda and eat all the dumplings in the house," the whip girl said.

Then the whip girl said to me how she, too, was beset with mischief, and if her uncle were here instead of back one day-turn toward morning away in Rainbow Mouth Park, then she would tell him to his face.

"I would steel-whip his ass off," the whip girl said.

That was the time when I watched the whip girl playing with the zipper on her jacket, pulling the zipper fast all the way down and up the front of her jacket over and over again, each time the zipper going down or going up, it sending out that noise that someone with a metal saw sends out when he takes his saw and takes his test strokes. Each time the whip girl pulled her zipper down, both sides of the part of the jacket which was above the zipper opened out in the shape of an arrowhead, and I was left watching for that time that the zipper was down and not yet pulled back up.

Later, I watched her button the snaps at the sleeve cuffs of the jacket covering up her wrists. The whip girl slung her purse strap over her shoulder, and hooked her thumb in the waistband of her trousers.

"You like melon?" the whip girl asked.

The boy who called me Gregor hung himself on her. The

boy was gripping a writing brush in one hand and a practice book in the other.

The whip girl pulled her thumb out of the waistband of her trousers and used both of her hands to pick the boy up. The girl's fingers were, it looked to me, like the legs of the sea spider.

That was the one time when it was that I wanted to be the boy who called me Gregor and to get caught by her as if I was getting caught by something that went swimming with me in the Southern Ocean.

I heard her say, "Okay, now this my baby."

There was a fat man who was the only one of them who, it seemed to me, made brushstrokes as if he really knew how to make them, besides the boy who called me Gregor, who did nothing mostly besides doing just that. But the fat man did everything.

"Boy," the fat man said. The fat man was talking to the boy who called me Gregor, calling the boy over to him to take a pin, to put it in the head of the boy who called me Gregor, to put it in and to twist.

The fat man lived in the back of the store that he sold his things out of. And the store was full up, because in it the fat man had everything he was going to sell, and the fat man was selling everything—The One Hundred Goods, The Four Necessities, The Sea of Ten Thousand Sciences, The Complete Book, The Old Books, The Crafty Pins, The Moxibustion Classic, and The Iron Man Balls.

The fat man was even selling what I was buying, which was the chance to sit in the back with them and to learn with them what they had left back in wherever it was that they, each of them, had come from, when their mothers and fathers had taken them over the ocean to here.

There was the time that I was looking through The Four Necessities and saw the practice book.

It was made out of tissue-soft paper that was nearer the vegetable state than any other paper I have seen. It was the color that you would get if you could turn a tree into dust and hang it in water. Each page of the practice book was folded double, so that you could put a practice card into the space formed from the two folded sides of the paper. Then, after you had a practice card in there in its place, you could trace over it with your brush to practice the ways to make the strokes.

The boy who called me Gregor was using his practice book, which was what that boy was always doing when I could see him.

Later, he put his face next to mine, very close. "You know," he whispered, "the fat man told me, from where we were in the South, they have a steel brush with a steel cap, and when you are done using it, you put the ink in the cap, and that keep the brush wet all the time, so the hairs can never dry wrong and not be pointed."

The whip girl walked by in front of me, her legs in tight black trousers touching together lightly with each step, the trousers-on-trousers sound like the sound of the steel wheel getting spun with its toothed edge ticking off against a peg of flint in a lighter.

The fat man left behind clean strokes in the practice book that looked to me as if they were strokes that could not be argued with. The fat man would keep his brawny wrist fixed, driven against the desktop, and would cut the brush over the paper, using only his fingers. Sometimes, I saw that that man did not even look at what he was writing on those soft pages. Sometimes, I saw that he did not even use the practice cards, but that he must have been writing only from his memory of how he must have thought the strokes ought to look when they were all down there together.

I saw the whip girl had walked over to where the fat man was sitting making his brushstrokes. The fat man moved in his seat to make a part of the seat he would not be sitting on.

The pigtail girl sang: Tuna-tunya, tuna-tunya, I love tuna.

The fat man hummed: Girl, girl, do not be angry. I sit on a chair, you sit on the floor. I eat melon, you eat meat.

Then I saw that the whip girl was not sitting anymore on the part of the chair that the legs of the fat man were not on, but had moved over and was sitting on one of the fat man's legs.

[4]

"Aunties!" I growled, "show me the way to take to the opposite other side."

The ones I asked said that first I would have to find my way to Rainbow Mouth Park. Follow Four Rivers North Road for a while, the sitters said.

Gold hair, small ghost, they said.

After I walked a little way off from the women, I squatted and shook my head to knock the sweat off.

It was nighttime when I saw it. Great floodlights were aimed down into the park, the salt-flake white light coming through the trees. I walked with my eyes on the floodlights. The panels gave a bright crystal glare and drew out bandy-looking ink shadows from tree branches, and drew out shadows shaped like horse ears from tree leaves on the dirt ground, on the concrete path. I could feel during the times when I walked between the lines and the bars of the shadows that the light was beating on my face.

After I had come through the stand of white-lit trees onto the midnight street, I stood on the road with a man who sold One Hundred Delight Snack. I bought kumquat soda.

Yah, yah, I give you cold.

Cold I have. Ice for keep cold.

Melon if you want, westmelon.

[5]

I watched a very tall boy pick up the boy who called me Gregor by the hair.

The tall boy fist-balled his hand.

I remember watching the lay of his shoulder.

I remember that I pulled him closer in to me by his shirt the whole time the tall boy was hitting me just under the lip on the chin.

The cousin of the tall boy asked me if I wanted to play Mahs or Dots. I pulled her pigtail. I told her one pull meant Mahs, two pulls meant Dots. I pulled her head back over the back of her chair by her pigtail so that her throat was bowed out, and I gripped her by her throat and said: "Marry me."

"How much you think I make, Gregor?" the boy asked me.

She tapped him with her long sharp one. "Honey, when you're in a group for life, they pay you five hundred sometimes per week," the whip girl said. "Don't talk to me about the fruit business."

The fat man whispered in my ear, "You can have her.

When I was going, the fat man gave me pins, practice cards, brushes, man root—"You needn't pay," the fat man said.

The tall boy who had picked up the boy who called me Gregor by the hair met me in the street. He was wearing a new shirt. I saw that the shirt was a turquoise one with no sleeves. I could see the arms of the tall boy all the way up to the tall boy's shoulders. The tall boy was wearing white trousers over his curved legs and black plastic-looking shoes on his feet. I saw the sunlight light him up—all the way from up on the tall boy to all the way down.

"Where are you going?" the tall boy said.

"What?" the tall boy said.

"Where did you say you were going?" the tall boy said.

"Give me that again," the tall boy said.

"Tell me, how is your face doing?" the tall boy said.

The east morning sun wested around the shoulder of the tall boy and shot a light-arrow into my eye. When I walked away from the place where the tall boy had put out his hand to shake hands with me for peace at last, I looked and saw that there was a scimitar of it in the air, the body-big white star of the reflected sun in the window of the fat man's place. I saw it as a great gout of firing white water, a window glass sending out the lash of a dotted blinding milk. **Q**

RICK BASS

Dennis and Probably the Rest

It's a mile down a gravel dead-end road to where I live. I live at the end. You go past only two other houses, getting there, and one of them used to belong to Dennis, before he moved away. The other house is my landlord's. He's an attorney, and so I've never tried any funny stuff. He could fix me. Though once, after I heard some especially bad news, the saddest, about a friend, I went slightly berserk. It was an attack of nerves. I took an ax out of the horses' barn and ran up to my house and started chopping it down. I started on the porch. The landlord could see this from his kitchen window; he was watching me chop down his front porch, the one I was renting.

Then, when what used to be the porch lay scattered all over the yard—my dogs had fled to the fields and were crouched in the tall grass, terrified—even the landlord, whose house it was that was being destroyed, knew better than to step outside or come down the hill to say something to me—then, with the front porch down, I ran around to the back and chopped down the back porch, and chopped the back door off its hinges.

I would have gone after the horses' barn next, but I went inside and smashed the kitchen sink, the dresser, the walls. I was thinking about Dennis; I was thinking about bad news. I broke the mirrors, the bookshelves, and then I started slapping the ax at the windows, winging it sideways like a big boomerang, bashing out the glass.

Next, I started in on the trees. I was swinging so hard that sometimes I would miss the tree and would spin around three or four times and fall flat on my face. The trees were hard to do. I could have leveled the house before I could have cut the trees down. It was hot and I was sweaty and bloody, and finally I just couldn't lift the ax anymore.

But it was still in my head, the news, and I knew that it always would be. It wasn't the first bad news I'd ever heard, but it was certainly pretty bad.

I live by a lake. In the mornings, I take a pitcher of coffee out to my white table down by the lake and sit in a canvas chair. Doves call across the lake. When the sun comes up, the bullfrogs start to drum. The horses look up every now and then, as if wondering why I exist. My dogs chase each other around and around the lake, running like greyhounds. They're black-and-tans, twins, sisters; they hunt frogs together, wrestle, chase butterflies. It's peaceful here. I use lots of cream and sugar in the coffee. I'll just sit there, feeling the sun off the lake, and listen to the doves. A few flies buzzing. Sometimes a fish jumps. There's peace. You wouldn't think that I crave peace. But I do.

I lived in absolute fear that the landlord would get back at me through my dogs, that when they were out of sight one day, or while I slept one night, he would knock them in the head. Even when you don't have anything, don't own anything, someone can figure out a way to get at you. They always can. They can get you. Sometimes the dogs would disappear for an hour or two, off running rabbits, and I'd go tearing up to the garbage dumpster a couple of miles away, and climb down into it and sift through all the rubbish, looking for their bodies. But the landlord never said anything about the Ax Day, nor did I ever repair any of the damage. I just pretended I didn't know how it happened.

I had a Zulu costume from a play in the eighth grade, a grass skirt and a wooden painted tribal mask and a spear, and some days, just to keep the fires of fear and worry burning in their own hearts, I would go out and dance in the front yard at length, making sure they all could see me, Dennis and the landlord. Then, the next day, I'd be as tame as a skunk. I might even wear a suit, and wander up the road to visit one of them.

Dennis taught over at the junior college. Some nights,

we'd cook out in his front yard, beneath the tall pines. He had Turkish coffee and Cuban cigars, and we'd string a bedsheet between the trees, and he'd show slides of Africa on it, which was where he and his new wife went each summer on some kind of trip. His new wife used to be just a friend, just another professor. But then they fell in love, I suppose, and she got pregnant. Dennis left his old wife, left his kids, and the new wife, who was forty, got rid of the kid she was going to have. Then they got married. She already had some other kids, too.

Dennis would tell me these things while we watched the slides and ate.

"Isn't this good?" he'd say.

Owls would be calling, back in the woods.

And "Have some more coffee."

But then I thought, If they killed a baby, what would they do to me or to my dogs? I was frightened. I locked the doors at night. I kept the dogs in the house. I could see the lights of his cabin, up the hill, at night, and not until his lights went off would I go to bed. I was running myself ragged with worry. If he would do that to a baby, then God knew what he would do to dogs for crapping in his yard, or to a man for just saying he didn't want any more coffee. I could bluff the landlord, but Dennis was crazier than I was. Dennis had the upper hand. He didn't care about anything. I thought about drowning him in the lake.

But Dennis moved away finally. My life is simple and easy again.

I say you've got to swing that ax. You've got to keep them all at bay. They are out there. They want you. Even here in a place like this. **Q**

Semper in Paradiso

I was born in the Garden of Eden with my grandfather's face, on the back flat streets of the God-forgotten coast, born in the bright body of the middle of the year, brought home to a dark house where I slept well at night. I was born in the farthest dark place off from when my sister was born and cried, and we slept in the rocking chair dark of my mother, near the Christmas-bringing bed—my father saying at night to my mother: She looks like the small glory of your father's old face, handed down. And I said to my sister before she could speak: She wants you to get up and walk so you can fall back down. And I thought the whole thing was the fall of life.

We lived on the level of the flat, half-gardened street, my father finding us at night with the lights on against the God Shall sounds of the coast and the whole dark for bed, and there were three leaning giants for us to bear when we said good night, if you counted the friend from the Portuguese past of my father—the one who changed his name when he left for Jakarta; and when he came back like a big Balinese bird, we were given a yen to say his name right, and his name by then was Mohammed.

My sister was born with my father's flat face and my father's black hair, my mother bearing herself like an eager leaning flower when my father found a card for my mother that arrived all in Latin that year from Jakarta calling my mother Voluptuous Sister. When my sister was planned like another small glory, they thought she would sleep like me and sleep well.

We built a booth out of chairs and we called it the Garden of Eden while my mother went out to vote, because it was called a booth where she voted—and floats in the Pacific Ocean, I thought, and thought she was casting the votes in her heart for Jakarta.

My mother and father did not sleep in the same dark Christmas-bringing bed, and when my mother went out for the milk, she never came back. When my mother came back with the milk after six months, she took the milk in the car and she took us, and my father read the part in the front of the car that reads miles and wrote something down in French for himself before we departed.

We made a new Garden of Eden in the back of the car with some blankets, then we kept the chairs in one place for the summer to hide in. My grandfather brought me a cake, because I was born in the middle of the year, in the bright part of the flame that was summer, my grandfather saying, It serves you right for touching something so hot, like an old man's heart, when I burned a way through my hand with his lighter.

When my grandfather said, It serves you right, I saw my grandfather's face look down like a bird going down for something in the river, and I saw the island the boys on my grandfather's boat would say later looked like their target before the boat where they slept exploded and burned, leaving a scar on my grandfather's head that looked like the island itself—or looked like Jakarta, my mother would say when she showed me. It was the summer we made a cave of chairs without placing a guard outside for my father.

My father came back for my mother, dragging the earth feet-first with his shoes, marrying my mother again in the shadow of some Balinese bird named Mohammed, in the shadow of the Catholic cross that was nothing more than someone's bent legs and bent arms pinned up like an old pterodactyl, my father said. And my mother saw the whole thing come true when my father half-handed her out of the car and saw how many miles it was she put on.

But there were no children and no cakes at the place, Just a garden for monks with a lot of purple mountains' majesty, my mother said; and my sister stood in the chapel of God with my father, and I wasted my knees, being bent. **Q**

He
became
irrational
while waiting
for the train

The Poet's Heart

I have always admired the Buddhist monks
who sat down in the middle of the road
in the middle of the war,
their white robes doused in gasoline,
and set themselves on fire.

I am in awe of the violence
of their immolations, the composed desire
for peace silently spoken to ashes—
the gift that endures
in the eloquence of their burning.

In deference to this,
poems, too, should burn
like a body on fire,
devoted, implacable,
not in flashing epiphany
but steadily, like the robes
of priests
and the world they could imagine.

And I think, too, of Shelley's drowned body
burning on the beach in Italy.
I think of Trelawny, who reached
his hand into the fire
to save the poet's heart.
The poet's heart: the poet's heart,
which the fire could not consume.

The Visit

My ex-wife blushed and unbuttoned her blouse
to show me her breasts, the puckered nipples,
and, what I most wanted to see and taste,
the miraculous thin white stream of milk
sputtering and shooting into the air.
Her white shirt open and loose like curtains,
she lifted her baby, offered her breast,
blind nipple in the V of her fingers,
and the child, quiet now, sucking, drinking,
held onto her breast with his greedy hands
until he fell asleep there, sinking deep
into the pure clear dark of infant sleep.
Then I held the baby and tried not to think
while she buttoned her shirt and fixed us drinks.

Mutability

On my European tour
I asked to see the building where I was born,
a small hospital on the outskirts of London,
only to discover it
no longer exists, is a field now,
a lovely small field of grass and flowers
surrounded by a brick wall.
When I walked the fields

at Birkenau, it was hard to say
what the rubble had been, buildings
destroyed and the remaining few stones softened
by weather and weeds. Wondering
how old the slender birch trees were,
I kept walking until I felt
concrete under my feet, and knew
I was in the chambers. I thought,

I'm strong.
I probably could have fought my way
to the top of the pile
of children and weak ones
and old people falling around me
in the Zyklon dark and lived
for a few extra minutes.

The place where I was born.
The place where they died.
And the place where I live now,
where I teach in America. There is a room

where I write words I want to share
on the blackboard, words to be erased
before I return the next day,
white dust on the floor, the slate washed clean.

A Shampoo

Letting your head go
back through my hands
and your shoulders touch

Water, letting my hands attend
the thick disorder
in great ladlings
is nothing if not love.

Enthroned, sunken,
slipping around
without ambition is a dream
of evil living

If not in a big tin basin,
then in this tub.
Lean back. Let me scrub.

The Creation of Eve

We lay a long time in the brine of my blood,

Father,
this other
            hacked from my flesh,

her side by my gashed side.
                              Strangers—

How fitfully we slept like that;
                              her hair
sponging the long cut just under my heart . . .

We didn't speak, falling asleep, waking each other
      in starts—

both feverish. Once I dreamed
you were calling and calling
                              and I
couldn't answer,
                  something caught deep in my
      throat—

It was days

before we could eat;
                        I split
a lopsided fruit and squeezed

the juice from its hundred
scarlet seeds
           into her mouth—

that's all she could take. So weak,
after being
           crushed into life in your hands . . .

I never asked

for another, didn't know
what to say to her,
           what to do—

The first three days we just
           gazed, not talking,
over the east side of the hill,
where you can see all four of the rivers

flowing
away from the garden
           (where
do they go?)—I laid
my head in her lap
           and she hummed,
and the sun

was dark by the slow-moving water;
we watched
three horned birds

I had not named
spiral above us,
black-winged and beaked, red-eyed—

My blood
still drained from the ragged cut; her skin
and mine were both stained,
and our hair—

like the sky, a red we'd never seen—
and the birds

splayed their wings and tilted
over us in rings, circling
down to the bloody

mulch of fig leaves where we

kneeled . . .

My Father,
I never thought
either of us

would heal—

Sleeping in Santo Spirito

Shut out
of Masaccio's chapel, where I'd tried
three times to see Eve and Adam

hunted by the angel, hiding
their genitals and eyes,
this afternoon I went instead

to sleep in the damp heat
of Santo Spirito. I watched
a priest in a black cassock,

swinging his silver censer, mount
the high altar to the Host
suspended among gold

to remake it into flesh.
Filthy, half-asleep, I thought
how the Gnostics wore black

to grieve
the soul's imprisonment in the flesh,
the light

buried inextricably in the dark body.
I watched him
consecrate and crack

the brittle tablet, dissolving it
bit by bit on his tongue,
mumbling

Corpo di Cristo . . . Hunched
low in my seat at the dim
back of the altar, I fell

asleep as the congregation
rose in communion, their hymn
resounding foreign

and hollow across the vaulted glass.
My body was fouled
with sweat: I'd walked

miles to see the *Expulsion,* and stood
spent before the scaffolded chapel,
its door

draped with a cartoon of the two
tormented figures. Aching
all over, I saw

that shut chapel again as I breathed
the holy smoke
of Santo Spirito, the votive

candles still burning
behind my eyes. The black
back wings of the stone angel

smeared into sleep, with the wooden
donation boxes for the souls
of Purgatory, only

the faraway wailing of the Mass
holding me up.
I woke to a black-cloaked monk

staring me down, his harsh
eyes accusing me of sickness
or sacrilege; slouched

over a dark pew
carved with gnarled
gargoyles, I was caught

half-asleep in the house of the Holy Ghost.

Outside Paradise

The scarlet berries and purple leaves of the pink
    dogwood in fall
surprise us. Across the porch,
the scrawny tree is fierce with color, impatient for
    spring.
Torn of their leaves, the cherry trees

scrape at the pink sky. In April they were laden,

skittering with bees, a thousand cherries borne on
    each limb.
It scared us, how we couldn't gather
half of them,
how they rotted on their stems, or split

and smeared deep red on the nubs of grass,

beyond our control, the way Paradise's
underbrush must have teemed, slithering
rubbery trunks, pond scum
breeding, sunflowers drooped into bloom, until
    Adam and Eve

would do anything it took to make it stop:

how they must
have flushed at the first
stiffening leaf, the wind
dragging the smell of the crumbling stems,

the richness of the fall instead of the rot.

The Night Venus Climbed the Oak Tree

It was another summer night.
Polaris had spitted Earth on his narrow beam.
One would have been hard-pressed to say
whether it was swallows in the sky
or the planet chirping on a rusting axis.
The moon stuck on a moth's wing
and fluttered like a feather out of sight.
Stars with trim athletic figures
floated like snowflakes on an updraft.

At ten o'clock Venus hooked a dimpled knee
over the horizon and heaved herself
into the oak across the street.
Her figure was not made gaunt by self-denial—
generous, strapping, lusty, bulging, fat.
I think she rued the burden of that amplitude
as she labored up the trunk.
She took two hours to make the climb.

What a pity, I thought, after all that work,
to turn at the top and come back down,
for surely nothing of her great girth
could rise like those weightless twinklers
up the dark. But when she reached
the topmost twig and leaf, without pausing
to catch her breath or admire the view,
she extended wiry appendages

in every direction and stepped off
onto nothing, like a sorceress levitating.

I wondered what it was that held
her up in such unfathomable fashion,
and it came to me that I was
lying at the bottom of a pool of night
and this squirming light above me
was nothing more than a water spider
skimming across the surface of the sky.
I knew then why those kings of old
had followed that other glutted star.
They weren't looking for a savior.
They were just curious how far
their spider of desire could ride
the tension before it fell.

Planting Cucumbers

It's been ten years since we buried
my father's ashes in a flimsy
tin box that must have long since
rusted through, mixing soil and ashes
indistinguishably. I think
I ought to plant a cucumber vine
on my father's grave. He always
liked a garden. The cemetery
caretaker wouldn't mind. Star-yellow
blossoms and large-hearted leaves
would decorate that place better than
plastic tulips. That cucumber vine
could put down hardy roots,
and Father's ashes could nourish them,
and I could pick those cukes,
and feed them to my children
and to my wife, Annie, who never met him,
and all our bodies would be richer
for knowing him this way,
and we could carry Father home with us,
and, best of all, some part of him
could stand again in light and air
the way a body was meant to stand.
Now what could be better than that!

Things

A telephone is ringing in the field.
The cattle circle it,
wondering if it will feed them.
When they graze away,
they leave a ring of flat seed heads
in the high wheat.

In the river, clothes are washing.
They rub against the rocks.
Sheets are weaving themselves
in and out of the current.
A red dress billows downstream.
A done shirt is spreading its sleeves
on a blueberry bush.

In the house the kettle is boiling.
Little steamy breaths huff over
the stove till all the water's
gone. Then, slowly, the bottom
burns. First red, then white,
then, through a rust-edged hole,
the first blue flame inside.

The Message of the Marriage Eve

The night before a lady is to be married, her attendants must search the folds of her wedding gown. If they find a spider there, the bride will be lucky in her married life. If not, the opposite conclusion is thought to follow.

These folds ripple white as Arabian dunes.
Do you see, Martha? Imagine that some trip
is taking place within, like the journey
our Sara prepares for tonight, that small
camels carry spices across the dip of her
waist, that a merchant waits for them
and their robed crew, satisfying his thirst
at a rare spring under palms. But Sara
shifts in her sleep, the camels tumble
to her bedchamber floor, the merchant drowns,
and we are left alone, with only a wedding
gown. We must search it carefully.
Should we miss the lady spider, Sara
may one day hunger, her husband lost,
dead of fever in the India of her dreams,
her children thin and begging in the street.
We must not fail. Here in the folds
of her sleeve I thought I saw . . . but no.
The dawn is coming, Martha.
The sun is coming on like a horse
through the mist. What do you say?
Shall we tell her we saw no spider?
Or shall we love her, and lie?

From "What Every Mother Should Know"

Oh, such a neglectful mother, Ann,
who left her child's first tooth, fallen,
to find its own rest, did not burn
the small bone as her mother told her,
did not fill it with salt,
did not ask God for a new one.
And a hen, wandering in the muddy yard,
pecked it up, with a worm and a wisp of hay.
So Ann's poor child grew a hen's tooth.
And cackles leapt from his mouth
at odd moments, for the tooth would not
be still. And he dreams, dear reader,
no longer of his mother's milk
but of yellow, only yellow.

How to Cut and Dry:
Study of a Marriage (1890)

With care, the hedgerows can provide a thrifty wife
with winter bloom. Most prized of all is honesty,
which may not be cut until quite dry
and must then be hung upside down in the dark
until its seed pods can be removed,
leaving only the white discs within.

It is so cold these days that my fingers stiffen,
reaching into the privet. This morning
I cut my wrist on some brambles,
but did not notice until the blood ran.
I have filled the house with winter's gifts.
In every closet something lies stiffening
between layers of old news. I have just
replaced the milkweed pods that used to stand
in a copper jug by the front door. They had
exploded, spilling seed across the entry. He
will not notice the fresh green limbs of pine.

The Pianist Who Keeps a Loaded Gun
on Her Piano When She Practices

The children know not to knock.
Double-sexed, I use both hands.
I tease seriously. The notes
tantalize, approach explosion,
fall back. It is the brink
that thrills when the high-wire
walker sets her pink foot
on the rope.
            The children know
I would shoot, but not at whom.
I am not certain I know myself,
only that this deep readying,
this fierce first step over
air, is worth dying for.

Mama DeBeauty Explains a Necessary But Uncomfortable Aspect of Dude Ranching

Darla and Allison DeBeauty
were fine-looking sisters.
They lived in the small
green rental
on California Street
and never quite shut
their blinds.

I could get on Dana's
shoulders and we'd
stagger from window to
bedroom window,
hoping for a chance
to glimpse something pink.

One Sunday evening, moments
before *Bonanza,* Dana
caught his foot in a
gopher hole and fell against
the side of the house
so hard
it rattled the kitchen china.

Well, when Mama DeBeauty
nabbed us by the earlobes
and shook us
against the clapboard
until our gonads
rattled like little seed gourds,
I pointed to Dana
and said in shaken desperation,

"My friend's in love
with your daughter."
Well, that changed everything.
Just as quickly as Little Joe
could mount his pony,
she had us both seated
in the living room
and proceeded to show us

photos of her father's
dude ranch
with stall after stall
of well-mannered geldings.

The Something Above Which We Share Below

When they painted the mortuary ceiling,
Chester wheeled out the only body,
and plastic was laid from corner
to red-carpeted corner. Each ceiling
tile was removed and handed down
from workman to workman,
dusted, stain-stopped,
and a slick white latex rolled.
By the time the last tile was painted,
the first was dry,
and so they went back up click click click,
like pieces in a rather elementary puzzle.
When the job was completed, the plastic
was wadded into a large ball
and tossed into an alley bin.
Then Chester wheeled back in
the only body. Its single lapel carnation
as white as the white of the ceiling above.

Dr. Cornish Hunts for a Screwdriver While Bewailing the Interdependence of Disciplines

In a corner of the file cabinet
in the upstairs bedroom
the screwdriver
has been wedged like a
file marker
between the phone bills,
office memos, and remodeling statements
of a Civil War historian
and a recently discovered record
of the Battle of Cow Creek.

The doctor insists
as he empties his toolbox
into a file drawer
that much like the screwdriver
the report was misplaced
for nearly a century,
the battle
allegedly occurring several
miles into Kansas
as opposed to Missouri

and was probably filed with the War Department
by some reconstructionist carpenter
who in providing new
office space for army historians
stuffed the report ineptly
in order to better organize his tools.

After Joey's Drug Overdose Dana Keeps His Memory Alive by Begging Cookies at Truck Stops

Dana would go in,
pretending to be retarded.
We'd call him Joey,
order his food, set
his silverware, and dab
his mouth with napkins.
He'd beg like crazy
for cookies, clapping
his little seal
hands and slobbering
his Sunday special
across the table.

Begging for cookies,
he'd prop
his head on the
booth behind him,
food crumbs drooling
into the lap of the
grandmother behind him.
Cookies, he'd beg the
neon diner. Cookies,
he'd beg the midnight
rednecks
bending coffee spoons
around middle fingers.
Cookies, he'd cry
to the flabby-armed
cooks and blue-haired
cash register ladies.
Cookies, he'd mumble

to a crooning Hank Williams
on the chrome juke.
Cookies, he'd beg
for Joey who was dead
and for the Joeys
who lived
and for the Joeys who were
caught
not knowing and cookieless.

And sometimes the waitresses
would feel sorry
and other times not,
but when they did,
they handed over cookies
like they were each
warm nippled breasts,
soft, hand-held, and dipped in pink.
But we'd step in
and give them back, saying,

cookies ain't
good for the boy.
He's got teeth in his head,
not gums.
And we'd leave him
cookieless
in the booth to pretend-cry
as we walked off into the gravel parking lot,
giggling at our joke.

Dana would rise
quietly like a family
man and pay the bill,
asking for his change
in just ones or fives, or some odd amount,
and he might mention how
last week's rain
was just something
perfect for the milo,
and then he'd leave
everyone blank
and speechless
like a dozen open drains,

and go floating off
into the night,
the way Joey did.

AL ORTOLANI

Frisbee Investigates the Angle of Love

When Frisbee's girlfriend
chose a woman to be her lover
instead of him,
he flipped
and took to driving
over to Galena and
jumping off of the chat
piles. He had a mathematical mind

and could calculate
the number of bounces
it would take
to keep
a fall from killing him.

He'd jump without fanfare,
unceremoniously,
slowing his descent
by bouncing
from ridge to ridge,

scuffing the gravel
into dozens of scraping
avalanches,
with all of us
looking on as silently
as plants,
assuming he'd lost
his mind as well as
his cherry,

146

in awe how that girl
must have been one soft cookie
to create

such a crumbling,
setting him up
to climb again
to the lip of the slope and,
before jumping, to mumble aloud,

"Maybe I'll get it right this time."

Urn

we put his ribbons on it
with scotch tape on the bar
      if you look close
at the photograph
you see the awards
but look closer at the corner
the blur
all the other pictures on the roll
have no such mark
but this one does
      not only has the blur
gotten larger and
changed shape
but it has also moved
      sometimes now when I look
I hear whispering
I expect soon he will talk
in a voice I understand

Rites de Passage

After we buried our grandmother
In the western corner of the basement,
We began to understand new names
For silences, but they were disturbing:
There were names that made us jump,
Like *sfeegkx* or *broasfi*,
Or names that came in raucous whispers at dawn,
Like *ukkakk* or *qiz'raf*.
We had never known
That silences could be so divisible,
Or that they could curve around your shoulders
And glove your skin
In clinging expectancies.

In winter we realized that
Grandmother had mastered every voicelessness.
We came to understand how all our talk
Somewhere else reversed itself, like steep
Tunnels of speechlessness beneath our sounds.
Our conversations seemed tinny with echoes.
Even our whispers had a gauzy clang.
Even our cries of love rang woozy as saws.

We felt some implacable intellect at work,
More powerful than all our grandmothers.

In late July we exhumed them, one by one.
With eyes averted and with urgent prayers
We consecrated all the eastern walls.

Now our speech has regained its ancient symmetry.

To Philip Roth

I'm glad to hear
You put Bucknell stickers
On your family's car
As a freshman
And took them off
As a sophomore
I'm glad to hear
It's possible to recover
From grave errors
Meanwhile
Me and my friends
We don't put stickers
On anything

Feeding the Ducks at the Howard Johnson Motel

I wouldn't say I was dying for it.
But he was already undressed, trousers, socks, shirt
in a heap on the floor. Now it's four in the morning
    and he
wants to feed the ducks. I tell him the ducks are
    sleeping.
The ducks are awake, though, floating
around and around on the pond
like baby icebergs. It's a wonder they don't freeze,
it's a wonder there aren't videos
in every room with ducks clouding the screens.

When I was six, my parents took me
to the Jungle Queen, family dining, with portholes
over every table. Fish swam past my nose,
dull-whiskered carp, shadowy
as X-rays. I tried to squeeze crumbs
through the glass, but now I think those fish fed
on one another. He saved bread
from dinner, and throws a piece to the biggest
duck, paddling in circles. Even the taste

of our bodies comes from so far away,
from bodies and bodies where we have washed
ourselves clean and hard as stones.
If a duck shuddered into him, it would
shatter. If my tongue blew away, I might know
what to tell him. Instead, I say, Why does the
    orange

bedspread look hideous when duck feet, the same
color, are beautiful? He throws again
and again, the bread sinking right

in front of their beaks.
I have been hungry so long I could
lift an empty glass to my mouth and savor the air
for hours. Each time I throw bread,
I feel like a child, my arm reaching out across
the pond, pitching as hard
as it can the fat balls of dough. Only
now I am aware of their dumbness,
their duck stupidity, how

they do not even see the bread, which glows
as it falls, every crust and crumb
shining under lights of the motel. Suddenly I
think of his teeth, hard
behind his lips; how, if a duck
bit me now, my hand
would open its heart, the rich
smell of something baking rising
from my flesh.

MAURICE EIDELSBERG

Poem

It soaks up
whatever
I have
to give
daily
whether I have
it
or not
and all I get
from this
one-sided feeding
is a little
green
growth
I can't even
see
and then
I'm left
drained

In 2s

They peck and paw
all around
me
in 2s
at tables
with no care
for what they are doing
to me
the only thing
I got
to do
is to watch
with nowhere
to go
for any
but they know
exactly where
they're getting theirs
and right now
they are using
croissants and
me
for their lovely
build-up

Pound

I'll go along
for handless walks
and no soft talk
do not worry
there will be
no fingers
in
or tongues
out
all I ask
is just once
you have to
watch me
pound myself
and see
what all this
behavior
is taking out
of me

The Quarter: Broken Elegy

In a meterless taxi she brings it up.
I can't talk about it. Not now.
The driver overcharges.
Why did I trust
this stranger, this moonlighter?
When the reluctant quarter he pours
into my palm slips under
the seat, I demand another.
The driver curses: "What's a quarter?"
I pull the seat, off and crouch
among the gray wadding.
Nothing shines there like a coin.
And the three-quarter moon rises over a park
brilliant and lucid and cruel,
the side of its face hacked away.
Vengeance? Whose?

And if I start
to think about
the child's death now,
when will it end?
It's dangerous:
going down steps
everyone is suddenly motionless—
a murmuring frieze
on the ascending escalator.
I don't know what to call it,
a place in the mind,
a hole, a tear, a gap,
the mind can only go around.

A fuzz around annihilation.
Waking and sleeping,
it impinges, ungraspable grief.

And in my dream the plane,
wobbling upward for a quarter mile after takeoff,
noses down into the warm ocean,
carrying loved ones,
and those not loved well enough.
Waking, the river stiffens with ice.
The rivers stiffen.
The fog splits off in jagged rifts.
Tugboats pass like hearses through the sluices.
And the joy, like levitation,
I feel near my son turns
to lead, then pushes like a steel bolt
through my bones, pins me down.
What do we have to know of hell
that heaven cannot teach us?
The quarter's gone.

Monks

Not for them these
airy, well-lit cathedrals,
places of gilt, of gold,
bishops in carmine robes
who would ride to heaven
in limousines;
for them it's
dark corners, small places,
ceilings so low
God has to stoop
to hear their prayers.

Revelation

Liquor is the song of the pharaohs;
it slips by his tongue like a psalm.
Moses on a three-day drunk again
comes back carrying
rocks instead of wages.
His wife can't understand
his lack of steady employment.
He says he talks with God.
She says he drinks too much.

I Love to See You

in the box of paper clips on my desk
it's a good place for you because I

can look at you when I'm telephoning
or typing a poem or putting poems in-

to the copy machine to send to magazines that don't want them   I tried

putting you in the little ormolu
frame where the daguerreotype of

Great-grandmother Henrietta used to
be but it didn't suit   you looked

too formal (you have lovely manners
but thank heaven you aren't formal)

so I pushed up the paper clips in the
box and leaned you against the heap

it can't be very comfortable (paper
clips are harder than hay) but you're

smiling away as if you loved it   I
hope you're also smiling because you

love me so much you don't care where
I keep you, even in the paper-clip box.

Bonanza

Do you remember the way the map of the
    Ponderosa would burn up?
Those demon teeth of wildfire working the
    weathered parchment.
That thrill;
always knowing everything'd be okay.

But Hoss is dead. Interned
in a purgatory of reruns
spliced with the irony of Lorne Greene
peddling dog food.
Another individual trapping the wild mustangs,
flexing the strong arm of the West.
Moral vagaries
separated
from the barbed-wire fence,
the rifle rack in the Chevy,
and the patch of lawn by the cistern.
And sometimes being right about it.
And sometimes not.
       Little Joe lifting himself
from the dust of Virginia City.
Adam resolute,
the princess's carriage disappearing
from the solitary high country,
land below already marked
by curling roads, heavy ranch houses,
the occasional wake from an outboard
crawling in an easy V
across blue Lake Tahoe;

the frontier converging
as dreams of prosperity-forever
blossom,
silent skull-blinding cauliflowers
rising over the roseate sands of Nevada.
Enlisted men crouched within an X-ray of skin.
Crouched within a disease of faith
in that white cross on the olive helmet.

Ben Cartwright shoveling against the flood.
Shoveling knee-deep
through the silt and tangled branches
of a land washing away.
Our shale of days washing away.
The whole show ending
in the miasma of seconds it takes
to raise a calfskin glove
and wipe the sweat
of our infernal transport.

Wedding Bells

My dad lost his job
during my sophomore year
in high school. Something
about younger blood
and a difference of opinion
on the battlefields
of mortgage banking;
cysticerci malls
perennial, larvae flowering
across Los Angeles's blond valleys . . .

But as far as I was concerned,
it was no big deal. Just
more time in the back yard together,
shooting hoops. Setting him up
with the double pump, then
releasing: the bulk of his chest
piloting me into the chain-link fence
at the top of the key;
nothing-but-net.

Afternoons closing
as he backs into the lowpost, clearing
the way with his elbows, pivoting: his shot
more of a toss toward the serene whiteness
of the backboard.
His dignity unassailable, remote. Burnished
    smooth.
A gift unwrapped and cherished
by the young-boy-from-Kansas-City-inside-him.
The young boy who stepped toward the lights

of the word of Jesus.   Whittling a poem
from those long days that must have added up
since his father entered that final Buick.
The farm girl of his young mother, holding
the photographs taken from the hand
of the detective.
Photographs of a black-and-white liaison
of betrayed ideals: Polaroid tribulation
for this wife who would never again
hear the soft repetition: Connie, Connie.

One man subtracted down the road to Texas.

The balance reminted in machines of forbearance:
coins traded for the kiss
between the milkman and the farm girl.   Coins
of a new type of courage.

That milkman's son
and the bride who followed him West
into a one-room apartment in Burbank,
finding their own corridor to salvation.

Spawning angels
among the blue lamps and gnashing teeth
of a white couch.

Each kiss the real bridge of grief.

Their fire permitting voyage:

                     Wherein,
the neon chapel is lit,
the minister speaks,
and we watch, spellbound,

as I place the ring
around the sweet circumference

that will someday be your finger.

Poem

Dear Hahn,

What was it that that English poet said? In every grain of sand a world? Please rest assured: your fantasy's no fantasy. It's barium, not radium. You've split uranium. Frisch, as you know, was in Kungälv with me. Like you, at first we thought it was a muddle. Then we went for a walk to work it out—or rather, *I* went for a walk. Frisch skied. A lovely day, which must have done the trick. We stopped, I drew a picture. "Couldn't this be it?" It, of course, was Bohr's liquid-drop. When it is hit by a neutron, it oscillates. A waist is formed, and then the waist gives way. You know the math. Two nuclei where there was one. The rest is pure Einstein. The weight of the two nuclei would be less than the parent by one-fifth of a proton's mass. Now factor that through Albert's $E = MC^2$, and you come out with what it takes to pull the nuclei apart: 200 MeV. And there you have it—all that energy. It's beautiful. Frisch says he feels as though he's caught an elephant by its tail. Imagine it: the energy from every nucleus would make a grain of sand begin to hop. What would our poet say to that? Two worlds for one. An elephant indeed. Or would a dragon be more apropos? Congratulations, Otto.

Lise

The Monastery at Rongbok

Outside, on the leaf-
strewn steps to the library,
works one whose

Faith is no less than
that of the translators and scribes
working inside the vaulted,

Candlelit rooms.
This one's instrument is but
a straw broom,

Tall as he is.
With it he writes his God-given
message

Across the steps:
Prepare,
for the hour of the year is late.

Basra

It was here, at Basra,
where they said the war
would be decided, two,
three months ago.

It was here where
the two armies massed
themselves, their jeeps
and tents and hangers-on.

The armies have met,
many have died, are dying,
and the fighting has moved
elsewhere in the desert.

At Basra, the women
wander the battlefield
and do not look beyond
the dead at their feet.

The Morning Mail

I gave myself the liberty to stay home
one Monday when I should have gotten dressed
and gone and pulled my end up like a man.
The house got empty after breakfast, which
was normal, though the house stayed empty
    weekdays,
excepting this one, where there was myself,
almost fanatical about the weather,
halfway determined to be under it,
listening for order in this nasty place
or words for persons not at this address.
After the mailman came and went, it was
the letter from a friend in Massachusetts—
pleading his right to special courtesy
from those among his fellow countrymen
who took the time to soothe him where it hurt
in the worn-out musculature of the soul—
making me lie back down in my bathrobe
to read for evidence of the common life
between us, with our other parts at large.

Outside was twenty years of waking dreams,
as of one rainy Monday in Joigny
at the Café République on the main square
where she kept stirring her café au lait
and glancing aimlessly over her shoulder,
wondering why we did this, but why we did
she wasn't to realize till we had crossed
the Alps to Domodossola and the lakes,
and there, in rain again at Sirmione,
she thought of how it was at home in Hartford

and why she had to go there one day soon.
Later that season, it was rain again
in Athens. Two old men in iron chairs
were leaning head to head above their beads
dangling between them, waiting for the train.
The sun came out in Yugoslavia,
after a rocking stop at Leskovac—
voices of crickets teeming in the corn.
I kept remembering that murky sunup
on the beach at Kalamaki near Piraeus
after a wakeful night. Down came two women
leading a blind old woman to the water,
and then the three of them, their dresses rolled,
stepped in the water while the old one cried.
Those are her daughters and they're bathing her
was the one thought that horrified us both,
to think of the Aegean as a bath of death,
these godly waters we took refuge by
in one another's arms, I said out loud,
already hearing voices in the room.

The letter dropped behind the davenport,
laden with pain beyond my reach. I said:
It's time to rise up and behold the day,
to stand beside the window and behold.
The usual blackbirds on my neighbor's roof
had come to shiver as the rites require.
They were three women, one of them a crone,
leaning together, elbow to elbow,
and one complaining, *Sister, she is old—*

MICHAEL HEFFERNAN

we need to take her up and make her fly,
and if she doesn't, maybe she should fall.
And what if they should tumble after her,
leaving their cries to falter in the quiet,
what would they be but black birds tumbling down
to drift above a neighbor's roof again?—
black angels veering in the atmosphere
to look us in our faces where we stand
like empty-handed lovers facing the sea,
wondering why we do this, and how those birds
could fall and keep aloft in the one air.

GREGORY H. JOHNSON

Paper Covers Rock

Paper covers rock.
Rock smashes scissors.
Scissors cuts paper.

The National Disgrace

"Is this the sex?" he said.
It was not the sex.
It was the violence instead.
It took him until the bullet
had stapled him to a tree
and passed out his neck
before he knew it had been the violence,
after all.
"It is not the sex," he said.
"Damn straight," the rifleman said,
ramming home another round.
The rifleman shouldered the rifle.
"This here is the violence," the rifleman said,
squinting down the long barrel.
The fellow touched his neck.
He could not feel where the wound was.
The rifleman shot him in the feet.
Both of them.
"How's that?" the rifleman said.
"Better?"

Love and Principle

When it was her day to drive,
she refused to stop the car
by the side of the road
to let her husband piss.
If she couldn't do it,
she said, neither could he.
The marriage died shortly
thereafter. Still, I
loved it. Fair is fair.

Last Saturday afternoon
I urged you into an alley
and tried to shield you
on three sides at once
while you pissed against
a wall. A guy started
up from the other end of
the alley, and I faked
nonchalance as I straddled
the stream flowing to meet
him, flowing downhill.

Weekend

[1]

Saturday, his doorbell rings. These guys come in with
a camera, lights, sound. They're from a TV station.
Let's see you having your coffee, they say. Pet the cat,
talk to your wife. He did. Look out the window, they
say. Hold these papers and look thoughtful. They follow him around in his bathrobe and slippers. They tell
him, sit in the easy chair, read the *Times,* make com-
ments. He did. They interview his wife. How did he
get this way? What's it like living with him? Then they
pack up, shake his hand, and leave.

[2]

Margie said it was cloudy. The clouds got lower and
thicker. They started coming in the windows. Her husband got upset. Shut the windows, he yelled, we can't
have clouds in the house. He turned on a fan. She got
a broom. But the clouds filled the apartment. They
couldn't see. Everything disappeared. They heard a
foghorn, heard seagulls. They couldn't see one another. Her husband yelled her name. She screamed
for someone to save them. She found the closet door.
She threw it open. The clouds rushed in and she
slammed it.

[3]

Marty is in this shopping mall. These guys come up
with a loudspeaker on a truck. They make appeals. All
aliens from space should turn themselves in. All run-
away children should come home. People who owe
money should pay it. People should open their homes

to the hungry, let the poor sleep in their basements. Countries should disarm. Everyone should turn in spare cash. Criminals should report to jail immediately. Fat chance, Marty says.

[4]

Ted had a great weekend. He went to Roosevelt Mall and bought walking shoes. He looked at pants, bought saddle soap, and had lunch at Burger King. He came out and found a couple waiting for him. They smiled. They followed him to Sears. They watched him buy a bag of washers and a box of fuses. Two women joined the couple. Ted smiled and tried to talk to them. But they were shy. They backed off. They followed him home. They stood outside his house. A tall guy joined them. They stood watch all afternoon. They were still there when Ted went to bed. He stood by the window and waved. In the morning, they were gone.

[5]

Lew went to his cousin Paul's house. It was time for Paul to die. Every year, Paul got a pain in his side. He got into bed and lay sweating, his eyes bugged out. The family came by. Paul confessed everything. He cried. Everyone said kind things. They patted his hand, kissed his cheek. They forgave him. Then he rolled his eyes back into his head and died. The family had a big meal downstairs. They drank and joked. Paul came down wearing a sheet. He was a ghost now. They ignored him. Even Lew did.

And Who Will Look upon Our Testimony

On an unsuspecting Wednesday in October 1347,
     A Genoese crew
"Who had sickness clinging to their very
    bones"
     Brought the black rats and fleas
Flooding into the Messina harbor
        On the northeast coast of Sicily.

The twelve galleys that landed had been driven
       By fierce winds
    From the East, infected and laden with spices.
      In three days the known world
Was changed forever by children
        Vomiting blood and howling for light.

It was changed by young Sicilian fishermen
      Who ran through town
    Screaming about the boils swelling in their
      Groins and under their armpits
Like blistering almonds,
       Like rotting eggs or apples.

The brackish blotches seethed and spread,
      Oozing blood and pus
    Until they turned into fiery purple knobs
     And peas sprouting on the arms,
Brittle black sea coals
       And cinders burning under the skin,

So that the stricken began to shiver and dance
        In strange bodily fits.
    Soon people were falling down in convulsions,
      Whirling through the streets
In a grim trance, and dying
        In the terrible ecstasy of fever.

A mother saw the face of death seated on the face
        Of her startled daughter,
    A father saw the emerald eyes of death glowing
      In his son's eyes. Doctors believed
That one coughing child
        Could infect the world's bloodstream,

And within months the continent was so bewildered
        And stupefied by pain
    That fathers abandoned their children, and
      wives
      Escaped from their husbands, brothers
Turned away from their sisters,
        And mothers denied their sons.

Peasants fled from their cramped hamlets and
      towns,
        Leaving the wheat uncut
    And the harvest untended, the sheep roaming
      Aimlessly through the countryside
Until they, too, collapsed and
        Died in the ditches and hedgerows.

Some people imagined a black giant striding
Across the land,
Others saw the Fourth Horseman of the
Apocalypse.
Some believed the plague had descended
In a rain of serpents and scorpions
When sheets of fire fell on the earth.

There were misty clouds, hot winds from the South.
A column of fire
Twisted above the papal palace at Avignon,
And in Venice the tremoring earth
Set the bells of St. Mark's pealing
Without being touched by calloused
hands.

The dancing went on. There were places where
"No one was left
To bury the dead, for money or friendship,
And whole villages scattered, like dust
To the wind." No one mourned,
Nor did the death bells toll.

"In Siena great pits were dug and piled deep
With the multitude of dead.
And they died by the hundreds, nay, thousands,
Both day and night, night and day,
And all were thrown into ditches
And covered up with the earth.

The people said and believed, *This is the end*
            Of the world!
    Blessed are those who did not witness
        The horror." Blessed are those
Who never fell victim to
            The dancing mania and the stupor.

The Welsh sang of death coming into their midst
            Like black smoke,
    Like a rootless phantom who cuts down the
        young
        And shows no mercy to the fair.
Woe is me of the shilling
        And the black pest in the armpit!

A clergyman recorded the death of five thousand
    sheep
            In one field alone,
    "Their bodies so corrupted from the plague
        That neither beast nor bird
Would touch them." Preying wolves
            Fled to the safety of the wilderness.

Some danced to the sound of drums and trumpets,
            Fighting the ghost
    With the high jollity of a happy music.
        Some kept carefully unto themselves,
Barricaded into their homes,
            Avoiding the grasp of the Evil One.

The Pistoian merchants decided the Dance of Death
        Was a warning from Heaven
    About crooked businessmen from Pisa and
        Lucca;
        The Circassian slaves thought the spots
Growing on their hands and necks
        Were a punishment from their masters.

And in the country the peasants died grotesquely
        On the roads
    And in the fields. In the cities, the rich
        Fled and the poor died in burrows.
"And everywhere men and women
        Wandered around as if mad."

The people believed that the boils were God's
        Tokens and stamps.
    In April, some friars saw the Star of Pestilence
        Exploding in the sky after Vespers;
In May, some nuns saw the Angel
        Of Death rising over the steeples.

And still the corpses kept piling up in the streets
        And the stench was foul.
    In Paris, five hundred bodies a day were carried
        In a procession of open carts
From the Hôtel Dieu
        To the cemetery of the Holy Innocents.

"And in these days was burying without sorrowe
and
            Wedding without friendschippe."
Priests bolted themselves inside of churches
        And died alone. And penitents in sackcloths
Wound through the streets
            Imploring the mercy of the Virgin
And hoping to appease Divine Wrath by sprinkling
            Themselves with ashes,
        By carrying candles and relics to the churches,
        By tying ropes around their necks
And tearing out their hair
            In acceptance of chastisement from
            Heaven.

The flagellants believed that God was punishing
            The world for its sins,
        And they roamed from town to town chanting
            Hymns and wearing cowled white robes
Emblazoned with red crosses.
            Some carried iron crosses in penance.

The martyrs gathered in a ragged circle
            In the town square;
        They stripped and scourged their naked torsos
            With leather whips tipped with spikes
While the townsmen followed,
            Groaning and sobbing in sympathy,

And crazed women smeared the blood on their
    faces.
                Across Central Europe
They were greeted as the frenzied redeemers
        Of Christ the Tiger, Christ
The Avenging Angel, who rose up
        And put his sword on their shoulders.

Soon they were rushing for the Jewish quarters,
        Trailed by citizens
    Howling for revenge and shrieking for blood.
        And thus began the lynchings
And the slaughter of innocents
        For poisoning wells and corrupting air.

Who will hear the testimony of eleven Savoy Jews
        Who were burned alive
    For carrying poison in narrow leather bags?
        Who will hear the cries of the Basel Jews
Who were burned in wooden houses
        That were built on an island in the
        Rhine?

At Speyer, the bodies of the murdered were piled
        In great wine casks
    And then sent cascading down the river.
        On February 14, 1349, two thousand
Jews of Strasbourg were burned
        In staked rows in the burial ground.

The four hundred Jews of Worms preferred to set
      Themselves on fire.
   And the Jews of Narbonne and Carcassonne
      Were dragged out of their homes
And thrown into the flames.
      No one listened to their cries.

"God is deaf now-a-days and deigneth not hear
   us."
      The chronicler said,
   "Things which should be remembered forever
      Perish with time and vanish
From the memory
      Of those who come after us."

The flagellants, too, dispersed, like night phantoms.
      And now no one believes
   That death is a black dog with a sword in its
      paws
      Or that pestilence darts from the eyes
Or that a Pest Maiden emerges
      From the lips in a clear blue flame

And flies from victim to victim. No one lights
      Smoke pots against her visit,
   Or falls down in terror before the wrathful God
      Of the leper and the bloated sheep,
The corrupted bodies lying
      In state for the starving dogs.

No one sings for the men and women who
    wandered
             The world in madness
    Or for the ghostly ships with their dead crews
             Or for the chronicler who died
In the middle of a
             Sentence about the plague:

"In the midst of this pestilence, there came
             To an end . . ."
    Fortunate are those who come afterward,
             The unfallen inheritors of earth
Who turn away from the Dance
             Of Death dying in the mind.

"Oh, happy posterity who will not experience
             Such abysmal woe—
    And who will look upon our testimony
             As fable." Oh, happy posterity
Who will die in its own time
             With its own wondering tales of woe.

Life in the World of Objects

The gunman had learned to stand
Back a few feet, past the splatter,
And this time that meant

He missed. The bullet swept
Through the man's hair, as gentle
As if it meant no harm, and suddenly

The woman was all over the man
Who had the gun, pulling him
Down, and the reprieved man took

To the others, and the three
Fell snorting amid the furniture,
A picture of Jesus on the wall.

Between thrashes, they breathed,
Gripped so close they smelled each other,
And somewhere in this partial embrace,

The gun held its own, like the other
Still things they had lived among,
Not ready, not quitting, not sorry.

One Summer I Lived by a Lake, Taught Poetry to Japanese Violin Students, Confessed My Adulteries

The water-skiers seemed crazy,
Coming so soon after, as if
To catch what pulled them,
Like analogies or caught fish.

And on the porch I would consider
Anything—a seventeenth-century silk dyer
In Japan, oblivious to John Donne
Making his poems on another island—

Anything but some man and some woman
Complicating each other, composing
Oblivions for the other, and the wind
Off the water might as well have been

Someone crying, for all the crying someone did.
My friend, un-French but having read history,
Went looking for the Bastille.
Cherchez bien, said the Gendarme,

Parce qu'elle n'existe plus. And me, too,
Ready to consider the years of practice,
The dark loops of windbreak
On the water off the far shore.

Big C

We drove around the valley, kissing like mad,
Looking for some water to lie down near—
No luck. Only the hellish hills,

The reservoir off-limits,
The river full of sludge,
No rooms at the only motel,

The pool formidable and fenced:
We went back into the heat,
Pent as teens. We went to the widow's,

Hoping she was gone. She was.
She'd locked everything tight and dry.
Only a bright space behind the garage,

So in the dust there, stung
And sweaty. She had a scar on her back.
I said, Who hurt you? She said,

Cancer. After that, we got out the hose
And sprayed each other, gasping
And dancing around in the widow's yard.

This Is Your Book

The father whose sons
are professors died. The father
whose daughters are pretty is ill.

The man who is over there is
my father. The house that I live in is
white. I am in favor

of approving it. I am fond
of my cat. I go to bed
early. I have

as much money as you do.
Whose is this book? The moon
is shining. The sun

is shining. I am washing
my face. I am about
to go out.

Without saying
anything. Without
saying goodbye.

all of his friends
became victims

—I want to be French, Hermione said.

—I want to smoke short, blunt, harsh cigarettes and write in pastel DuPont ink, said Gwendolyn.

—I want to be a princess in a tall blond tower and let my raven hair down for a chartreuse knight to ascend and lend my state an air of dignity, said Giselle.

—How happy are we, said Perry.

—A statement, said Phyllis, stepping off the plane.

—I want on the same day at the same hour to receive postcards from everyone I've ever known with the same message: *I love you, Prissy.*

—Redundant, said Perry.

—I want all the stamps to be different and exotic, said Prissy's twin.

—I want this room to be suddenly filled with flowers, their scent like the burning coal of a cigarette.

—A Gitane.

—I want my Saab to purr smoothly, as it did in our youth.

—I want the speaker to identify himself.

—To step out from behind his arras.

—To take on the manner of the farm boy.

—Just coming into his own sexuality.

—Fresh as morning dew.

—New-mown hay.

—Outside, out from behind the barn, I mean.

—Standing outside Saks, I saw, I saw a man who made me tremble. Are any of you able to remember the last time a man made you tremble? A man of such poise, of such coiffured refinement, of such elegant noblesse, of such a twist of lime, shaken not stirred, that I, I a woman of herself such elegance, that I was there, on that spot, not fourteen paces from the perfume counter, the best, most splendid perfume counter on the Eastern seaboard, taken aback. Utterly.

—The last time I trembled, Giselle said, was on one of those cold rainy winter afternoons in the chemistry lab with the pungent glow of the Bunsen burners reflecting their tulip flames in the Erlenmeyer flasks and the sound of pure chemicals bubbling and gurgling like a baby's sleep and Faber #2's scratching notes in the soft woody body of workbooks, the sound of small furry bodies in moist wood.

—What happened next? Prissy said.

—Prissy's twin said, I fell down some stairs and twisted my ankle or I twisted my ankle and fell down some stairs or when I fell down some stairs I twisted my ankle or when I twisted my ankle I fell down some stairs or as I approached some stairs the possibility of twisting my ankle suddenly became a reality or the possibility of twisting my ankle was suddenly realized as I came upon some stairs or the reality of twisting my ankle suddenly became a possibility.

—The time, said Hermione, is our guileless youth.

—My occipital is piqued, said Perry, femurishly. I am led back to a more masculine emotion, banish woodsmoke and eglantine, all words dew-scented, tear-dropped, pear-shaped, and similarly hyphenated, embrace, said Perry, the sweat and ordure of sphincter, ligament, tendon, and testicle, of exertion, of excretions great and small, of gray towers rising through sexual seraphic skies.

—O lost! shouted Prissy's twin.

—O faint spell of remembrance, more to the point, said Hermione.

—O sweet Jesus, Marcel, opined Gwendolyn.

—Fill my glass, said Prissy, pouring anisette all around.

—O paean to faded ambiguity, said Phyllis.

—And Bess was Bess, said Bess, joining the group.

—And demeanor was not all, said the gathering in unison.

—A pause, a lull, dispiritingly settled.

—We have sunk into effete snobbery, mindless locutions

of mundane nihilism, diverting not in the least, said Bess, the sturdiest assembled.

—We are in need of the center, interrupted Perry, removing his shirt, airing his tattoo.

—We are thugs, demons of night, street people, vagabonds, with all our possessions in our pockets and rolled in our sleeves, said the tiny university-trained Giselle.

—Statements, said Phyllis, thinking of her father's oil fields in Louisiana.

—It's a great stinking parable, idn't it, luvvy? said Giselle.

—Where does this parable occur? said Gwen. **Q**

To make things simple, we'll start off with even numbers. If you get an order for a thousand 130 by 29—that's in millimeters—first you multiply 136 times 29. You add on the six millimeters because that's what gets cut off when you get to the skiving machine. So that comes to 3944, the number of square millimeters in the apron. Now divide that by 645 and you'll get the square inches: 6.1147. Now multiply that number by a thousand, for how many aprons you'll need, and then divide that number by 86—the approximate number of usable square inches in a square foot of calf skin. My father figured it out. It's always been 86, through good and bad tanning periods.

Now you know how many square feet of calf skin to use. About 72 feet. A little over four average-sized skins.

Take each skin to the stripping table. It's about six feet long, has a long, thick metal bar on top with a sliding razor handle in the groove of the bar. The back bar should be set to seven-and-an-eighth inches, because when you get to the dividing machine you'll need to get six aprons per block with three millimeters, more or less, trim to each of the blocks. Different apron widths, of course, require different settings for the stripping table. You'll have to figure out the math for each, maybe write it on the wall behind the machine.

Strip each skin. Don't step on the foot pedal with your thumb underneath the bar. It'll flatten it out, make you a better swimmer, hurt like hell. You won't be able to know to step off the pedal, that's how bad it hurts. Skive the bastards. Sweat on them so they know who's boss. Put a lap on the front and back sides of each block. Don't put two on the same side. The geezer in the mill will try to lick and stick it, and it'll turn out looking like a Möbius strip. No good in the cotton mills.

Don't get your fingers caught in this machine, either, you know. You can either glue the blocks' laps, or do them one at a time after they've been divided. Basically, you want a thick, even coat of glue *just* on the laps. It takes a lot of practice. You have to learn how to fan the blocks out, each block to the edge of its lap area. When they've dried, go to the dividing machine. My father rigged up this old printing press, made up a slew of die cuts for most of the widths used in the mills. If some cotton mill wants something odd—like a 22-millimeter, or a 57—you just have to make the block yourself, using shims, blades, and butt slugs. You don't want to get your hand caught in this machine, either, or it'll first crush it, then cut it into seven pieces. Unless you're working on 142 by 44s. Then you'll only get cut five times. Inspect each apron. Any one with a scar on it, no matter how minute, is no good. Stack the good ones into fifties, wrap them in cellophane, mail them off UPS to the mill.

It's impossible to write out how to make a replacement apron. Whenever I mention it to anyone, they think I make leather things for people to wear in the kitchen.

Don't be afraid of the splitting machine, either. But don't get your sleeve or finger caught in the feedrolls. There's a thirteen-foot band blade rotating, but enough safety guards. I think. Maintaining this dinosaur is hell, and I'm one of the few people left who know how to change the blade. I learned the hard way, after Dad died. We used to have a newer model, but it didn't work as well as this 1936 job. USMC stands for United Shoe Machinery Company. Somewhere up north. They'll charge you airfare and a hundred ten bucks an hour to come down and fix it. So it's cheaper just to figure it out yourself, make parts when necessary.

Feed each strip of leather into the machine. It'll split them down to .050. Or .038 if that's what the mill wants. Adjust the feedrolls up on the top to determine the settings. But you'll have to experiment, waste a piece of leather or two. For some reason, the settings seem to change when no one is here for a couple of months.

Take all of the split strips over to the old skiving block and, with the wooden-handled razor, cut them into blocks 136 millimeters long. The block used to be used to skive, but it's too time-consuming keeping the skiving blade sharpened and hollowed in the center just right. Now we use the automatic skiver to put on the laps on each apron. Kerouac's mother ran one of these things up in Massachusetts at the shoe factory.

Now take the blocks to the automatic skiver, make sure the foot of the thing is down and set for .050 leather.

I started learning the business when I was twelve.

My father made me. Q

He was so sick, so sick. It was brutal. These last eight weeks he could not walk. We had been in and out of the hospital five times since June. This last was his last, and him so hurting. He died Sunday, January 10. There were no more positions for him in the bed. We moved from side to back to side again. Everything hurt. I forced food on him, then his throat closed up. Oh, it wasn't fair—he was so good, so good to me, he was what has been all highest in my life. He thought I didn't know, so he wouldn't tell me: he kept taking care of me even when he was all pain. Oh, God! The funeral, six hundred people, everyone who had ever worked for him, all his cardplayers, old friends from high school, flew in from Florida, from New York. He was not social. He never made a phone call. He was just good, and everyone knew. The kids and I, Grandma Shirley, his two brothers, we were all with him at the end, on the bed with him and in the room. He is in a cemetery in the South Side slum where we both grew up. We used to climb over things there and play there when we were kids. Will wear my torn black ribbon for a month and cry for missing him, then will go on alone across the field. Here are the things my kids wrote and read for him. *When they found my father's cancer, it was in his kidney. The kidney was removed. Then it was in his lungs. Then his brain. This week it moved to his heart. The doctor cried. My father died Sunday. The last words he said to my mother were "Shall we close the book?" My mother answered, "Only if it's too hard to keep it open." They told me tumors in the heart are only found at autopsies. My father kept the book open as long as he could. These last six months my dad was cut, he was poisoned, and he was burned. He never complained. He never cursed God. He died the same good man he lived. Dad, I will always love you.* **Q**

In the spring of the year after I was born, Vachel Lindsay ran an ad in a literary review inquiring, in Vachel's often inflated and dramatic style, if there was anyone out there who would care to exchange bread for poems. My father at once answered in the affirmative—and I believe his was the only response which Vachel received. Father enclosed a train ticket (coach) from Gulfport, Mississippi, to Spokane, Washington. Vachel packed up his hundreds of books, notebooks, scrapbooks, and manuscripts in Gulfport and in Springfield, Illinois, and shipped them to the Davenport Hotel. Privately, Father had made an arrangement with Louis Davenport, sole owner and proprietor, to house Vachel in a pleasant suite of rooms on the top floor, charging him the nominal sum of thirty-five dollars a month, Father to contribute the rest from his own slender pocketbook, unbeknownst to Vachel.

It is worth a moment's digression to speak of Louis Davenport, an unusual man even if this were all that we knew about him. In the great Spokane fire of 1889, which virtually destroyed the city, young Louis Davenport (I believe that that was not his name then; it was something Armenian) had set up a tent and a flapjack stand on one of the ruined blocks and was doing a thriving business feeding the inhabitants, including miners, lumbermen, their families, prostitutes, and assorted scalawags. Legend has it—Mr. Davenport's legend, anyhow—that a gypsy fortune-teller showed up and insisted on reading his palm. "You will be *vairy* rich and successful," she said, rolling her gypsy eyes, "if you build a hotel on this *vairy* spot, so long as your hotel is filled with singing birds, living fish, water fountains, and fresh flowers."

And so it came to pass. The Davenport was an amazing establishment for the small-town America of that day. As I was growing up, it was in its prime: Between the pillars in the lobby were hung cages of beautiful singing canaries; fires burned all day in the massive fireplaces at either end of the lobby; and in the center was a large fountain surrounded by masses of living blooms. (It is significant that the hotel prospered until Mr. Davenport died, the hotel was sold, and a series of subsequent owners eliminated the birds, the fountain, the flowers, the fish in their tanks, and the fires in the fireplaces. And the hotel, growing ever shabbier, has been in trouble ever since.)

When Vachel moved into the Davenport, all coins that passed through the hotel were washed and polished until they gleamed like new. Every incoming guest received flowers and a basket of fruit. Vachel brought with him one of his own large paintings, entitled *The Tree of Laughing Bells,* which Louis Davenport hung in a prominent place on his elegant mezzanine.

Every Sunday morning, my father would walk from our house at 202 Coeur d'Alene, right at the end of Second Street, all the way down to the hotel, where he would pick up Vachel. They would walk for hours, along the banks of the Spokane River, or on the Rimrock, overlooking the valley. Vachel, an enthusiast if there ever was one, was at this time infatuated with the architect and medievalist Ralph Adams Cram and Cram's concept of "the walled town," a utopian city whose ramparts would shut out invaders. Vachel fancied that Spokane, surrounded by rocks and scrub pines and fields, could be such a town. Vachel had had his dreams of Springfield, his hometown, but they had come to nothing. Now, perhaps, if Spokane could be made to listen to Vachel as he preached his Gospel of Beauty to men's clubs, the Elks, the Chamber of Commerce—whose program directors, always desperate for luncheon speakers, particularly those who charged no fee, were happy to invite Vachel to speak—if Spokane could be made aware of Beauty, then she might approach the ideal of Cram's and Vachel's fantasies.

When I was barely able to toddle, I sometimes accompanied the two men. There are snapshots of the three of us in the family album, Carolyn self-consciously holding up one Mary Jane-shod foot. Vachel had told me that I had "Della Robbia toes." I had no idea what kind of toes these were, but they sounded special, so special that I thought they might be visible through my shoes. The snapshots help to restore my memories (though I believe that they also suppress the genuine visions in favor of the printed ones). But I truly remember Vachel's great gusts of laughter; it was an extraordinarily loud, braying laugh that must have echoed for miles across the valley —and his nonstop, uninterrupted discourse. What a talker the man was! I have noted with indignation that some accounts refer to Vachel as a drinker. Nothing could be further from the truth. Like Father, he never took a drink in his life. But unlike Ben Kizer, Vachel never outgrew his puritan origins. It's understandable that people might think that he drank, because he became intoxicated by his own language: his voice would rise and rise until he was shouting. I don't remember many of the words, but I will remember the tones until death silences all.

One night Percy Grainger came to the house. He had known my father for some time, Father being chairman of the symphony board and responsible for booking the artists who appeared with it. It was always exciting to have Percy visit. Like Vachel, he was a highly dramatic, even florid, personality, though far more attractive than Vachel, who was, in truth, a plain and gawky man. Vachel believed that these qualities made him resemble his idol, Lincoln, though it is difficult for an objective outsider to see the resemblance. Percy would appear for dinner, dazzling in white tie and tails before his concert, and would insist on clearing off the table between courses. Percy protested his democratic spirit in all things, to the consternation of a succession of German maids who would fall back against the walls when Percy swept into the kitchen with a pile of plates.

On this particular night, Vachel, Percy, and my parents had been to a lecture by a young Englishman who had recently returned from Africa, where he had studied tribal drumming. He came back with them to the house, and I was permitted to come downstairs in my Doctor Dentons because my mother believed that children should be included in Special Occasions, which were more important in forming the infant sensibility than Regular Hours. There was an enormous fire blazing on the hearth, and the young Englishman was sitting cross-legged in front of it with an assortment of drums. I remember his quiet voice as he began softly, tentatively, to drum. Suddenly Percy sprang to the piano and began to play his "Zanzibar Suite," recently composed. In a moment Vachel leapt up and began his chanting:

> Then I saw the Congo, creeping through
> the black,
> Cutting through the jungle with a golden track . . .

All the lights had been turned out, and Vachel's face blazed in the firelight.

> Mumbo-Jumbo will hoo-doo you,
> Mumbo-Jumbo will hoo-doo you,
> Mumbo-Jumbo . . . will hoo . . . doo . . . you.

All my life I have lugged an old blue silk hatbox from one to another of the places I have lived. In it, along with my grandmother's, my mother's, and my own christening gown and other antique treasures, is a tiny Bible. In it, Vachel has inscribed, in his characteristic scrawl, large, round, and black, *To Carolyn, from the man who usually writes on barn doors, but can write on an angel's penny.* And somewhere in every house I have owned are some framed drawings, product of Vachel's "word game." This entailed Vachel writing out the signature of the person in question, and then turning that signature into a portrait. My favorite is Elizabeth Barrett Browning, ringlets and all, a dead likeness. Vachel would have loved to have been an artist, and he kept coming back to drawing for all of his fevered life. But his gifts in this genre were limited, and most successful when linked to literature, as with the word games.

I think that people have been inclined to overestimate Vachel's influence on my becoming a poet. I think that from a very early age I sensed Vachel as a man frighteningly flawed, a man stubborn, obsessed, blind to the realities of the crass American towns where he sang his songs and preached his beliefs, whose citizens laughed at him and thought him a buffoon. And who ultimately destroyed him. No, the chief influence came from another direction. Vachel had a sister named Olive Wakefield, a missionary in China. I remember Vachel reading her letters aloud; I remember Mother saying that Vachel wrote what was, to her, his best poem, "The Chinese Nightingale," on our living-room sofa. I remember Mother reading aloud to me the translations of Arthur Waley. Through Mother, and Vachel, and Mrs. Wakefield, whom I never knew except through the excitement which her letters caused, I acquired my unending devotion to Chinese poetry.

Of course, Vachel was a limited poet, limited in some of the ways in which Sandburg was, and for some of the same reasons: they were both obsessed with the idea of being American, a kind of crippling chauvinism which blinded them to the importance of what was happening in Europe: the French symbolists, Eliot, Pound. But even with his limitations of judgment, and I suppose ultimately, of talent, I often wonder what Vachel's life would have been like if he had been born forty years later. By the time he was grown, the Main Street Babbitry of small-town America would have diminished; poets no better than he would read poetry to jazz in San Francisco clubs to wild acclaim.

I remember Vachel's answer to a reporter who asked him how long he planned to stay at the Davenport. "Till the ants carry me out grain by grain through the keyhole," he said. **Q**

Let's talk one more time about Vern's divorce: the one where his wife stripped him to his shorts and drove around town with him lashed to their hood like a field-dressed deer.

The one where he lost his children, his health.

The guy I know used to freeze his whiskey, like Hemingway, before drinking it in the winter.

But now: now! Are you kidding?

He drinks it from the bottle now, my friend Vern, and in the summer he sweats like Hemingway, and that's it.

Vern's pushing forty.

Two more weeks.

It's been two years, and still he moons about the vexations of the divorce. He shuts his eyes a lot, or puts his hands over them when he speaks of it.

I like to probe. I like to try to keep it from being buried, covered with sand, washed over with time. I'll ask him questions, questions about the old Vern I never knew: just this new, sweating, shut-eyed Vern.

It's broad-ass daylight outside, clear summer Sunday skies, and Vern's sitting in his dark low little apartment. That woman has ruined him.

What color was the wedding cake?

Huh?

The day you two got married—tell me about the cake. I want to know what it looked like and what she looked like.

Ohhhh, ohhhh. He'll clasp his face and moan again, maybe lean forward and tumble out of the chair.

Or I'll make up things, which, in Vern's sweat, he thinks he remembers.

You used to go canoeing with her on the lake at night. You used to take showers together. You used to share pizza.

Shit, he mumbles, rubbing his face with his hands. Shit, shit, shit-damn, Vern growls, remembering, or thinking he remembers.

You took roses home to her. You loved her in the front seat of the car.

Yes! Yes! he shrieks, pulling at his hair, penniless, doomed, finished.

That Vern, he is a lucky son of a bitch. He had it real good once, and I am here to remind him. **Q**

It's O.K., I have
this caster.

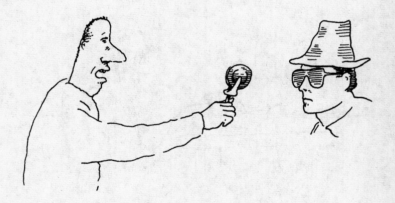

Listening to bugs .

NO, IT'S TOO SKULL-BORN

cleaning the sleep

L a u n d r y

BACK of the NEW

Concrete, lead and wood
racing machines
30' long   15' high   40,000 lbs.

Rubber Boats

2 man	38.00	16 man	177.00
4 man	56.00	18 man	214.00
6 man	72.00	20 man	239.00
8 man	87.00	22 man	267.00
10 man	104.00	24 man	291.00
12 man	132.00	26 man	329.00
14 man	169.00	28 man	372.00

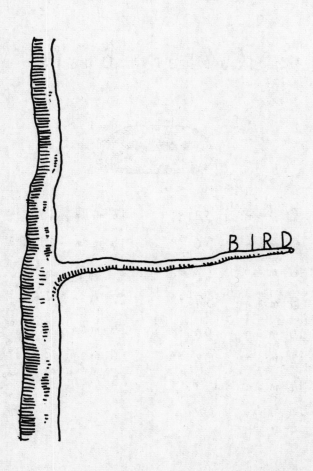

DAVID CANTWELL SCHER

the finest of cheeses

D. C. S.

This went on all night.

I would be nodding off, and hear him say, "What time is it?"

I would unfold myself from the recliner in the corner and move to the side of his bed. The room was dark except for a thin neon light above him. It illuminated his face perfectly. I would glance at the clock on his bedstand. My mother had bought it for him the day before I flew in. It had a white face that glowed in the dark.

"Twenty after eleven," I said one time. "It's twenty after eleven."

"Oh," he said, and then he brought his head up to look in the direction of the clock. He was looking past it, toward the wall. He set his head back down again.

"Is there anything I can get you?" I said.

He shook his head.

I turned away from him, back to the chair, and he said, "It's hot in here."

I looked at him. "You're too hot, Dad?"

He pointed at the far wall where the thermostat was. "See what that says," he said.

I went over to the thermostat and read out the setting to him. "Seventy-two."

"Turn it down," he said. He moved his hand to indicate the direction of change. I spun the dial to sixty.

"I turned it way down."

"Good," he said. "Good."

He brought his arm down to his side and closed his eyes. I stood at the foot of the bed. One of his feet was covered by the sheet, and I knew he did not like that. When the nurses came, they would tuck him in on all sides. After they left, he would motion to someone, my brother or my mother or my-self, to get his feet out from under.

I carefully pulled the sheet off his foot and folded it back to his ankles. Mary Magdalene washed Christ's feet with her tears. She kissed Christ's feet. I kissed my father's, and cried in the chair in the corner.

This went on all night.

My brother, P.J., was asleep in the waiting room. We were all waiting. My mother was home, sleeping. She would come back at six o'clock in the morning. The chair I was trying to sleep in reclined to one position before being blocked by the wall and the window. There was no room to pull it out farther because it would interfere with the nurse's getting around my dad's bed.

His breathing came in gulps, and he would start awake every ten minutes or so, his eyes jerking open before they fluttered closed again. It was as if he were a child alone in a strange house, a strange bed. It was hard for me to sleep because I would not know when he would wake up and need something. I prayed, "God, let him sleep," so that I could, too.

There was a horn blasting down in the parking lot. I got up and looked out the window, down onto Harbor Boulevard. It was all lit up, the Dal Rae Restaurant, the Mobil station. Off to one side was the Boys' Market. I'd walked to the market that afternoon to get him some half-and-half. They didn't have any in the hospital, just milk and some creamer they would use in the coffee. My father wanted half-and-half. It was a hot day, and I remember thinking, This may be the last time I go to the market for my dad.

I brought it back and it didn't taste right to him. Nothing tasted right to him. My mother had one of the nurses put it in their refrigerator. My brother just stared at me.

We rode bikes, me and my dad, down Brea Boulevard, through that old section of town, then across to Harbor. We rode all the way down to Hillcrest Park. My dad told me he used to bring my brother to Hillcrest Park when P.J. was just a boy, when he was still going to St. Catherine's. My dad and I had brought sandwiches with us, two apiece. Cold hot-dog sandwiches, the weenies split down the middle, the long way, then in halves again. There was mayonnaise and mustard and catsup on white bread. We had brought potato chips. My dad had packed everything in a brown bag and strapped it on his bike rack. We bought cold sodas at a market near the park.

That was the first time I had ever been allowed out of our neighborhood on my bicycle. I rode in front of my father the whole way, and he would yell up directions to me as we went along.

He said something, but I could not understand him. I stood beside the bed and touched his hand.

"What is it?" I asked.

He looked up at me. I don't think he knew me.

"Huh?" he said.

"Are you okay?" I said. "Do you need anything?"

He shrugged and turned his head on the pillow, looking away from me. I squeezed his hand.

"Cold, Michael," he said.

"Do you want me to turn the heat up?"

"Okay, Michael," he said.

I turned the thermostat up to seventy-five.

"It's up now," I said.

I pulled his blanket up over his chest.

"Hi, Dad," I said.

I could feel his fingers trying to squeeze mine, and I held them very gently.

"Sleep," he said.

"Go to sleep," I said.

He pointed past me and I turned to look. He was pointing at the chair. Then he tapped the back of my hand.

"Okay," I said. "Do you need anything?"

He shook his head and squeezed my thumb.

"What time is it?" he asked me.

I checked the clock.

"A quarter after twelve," I told him.

"Oh," he said, and rubbed his chin. He looked toward the window. "It's late," he said.

"Yes," I said. "Can I get you anything?"

"No." He touched his forehead. "No," he said.

His arm dropped to his side and his eyes closed. I watched his chest until I was sure it was still moving, then I tried to make myself comfortable in the corner. **Q**

My dog's not company. I have city people over, good ones I deserve to meet. I serve them salty things on these flat crackers which nobody eats. After they leave, saying they'll come back soon, I give it to him hard. He whimpers. He was a present from my father.

For years, during the holidays I did everything. I was the smallest and licked frosting and hung stars and laughed late at night. He, Father, said, "That'll change," and I asked why and he said, "Wait and see." For a while, he came across as wise, then foolish, and then later: he was right. Without trying hard, I had a baby, had to live home a lot longer than was good.

They loved each other a lot in the car, my parents—they'd touch, chin on shoulder or hand on knee. And talk nicely, too, as if going forward as driver and passenger was easier than eating at the same table. I sat in the back with my big sister and brother, me in the middle. Rat-faced boys with braces would ride by on their bikes, staring down my sister, but it was me who remembered them. Later, when I was still the smallest, I went with them into cars, where a lot happened quickly, and my father was not surprised.

One week my baby was quiet, and I'd say, "Grampa, what a quiet baby we have," and he'd say, "Next week he'll be screaming." And the baby would. Or my baby would be neat and not even need a bib and my father would say, "Just wait until he starts spitting up." Soon there'd be eggs and carrots everywhere. Once we were looking at TV and he said, "Pretty soon you'll be bored with all this," and I was. Right in the middle of a commercial I started packing. As I left, I shouted, "You're so smart, you keep the baby!"

My father said, "I knew."

I lived in the city for a year before I called home crying. I said, I miss things, and he said, "What about your baby?" and so I said, "Him, too."

"I'll send you something to hold" was how he ended our talk.

That was when I got the dog. The dog came in a box with holes and he moved around a lot, and for a minute I thought it was my baby. And I could picture him sitting at home, holding the baby, and laughing at me for thinking the wrong thing, even for a short while. So that's when I started hitting at him. Never hard, just to surprise. Not every day, just when there were new neighbors who didn't smile at me and I thought of calling home.

When I finally do, and he says, I think you'd better come back, well, my bags are already packed and I like that finally I get the last laugh. Then he says, "And bring the dog—he can't live in the city." So I leave him, though I was planning to take him all along. Q

She is not always predictable. Some mornings she runs her bath at 6:45, other mornings fifteen or twenty minutes later, and I am kept waiting in the dark. I don't know which I prefer—the growing excitement of the long wait or the sudden gush of water when I'm hardly awake, still half dreaming . . . as she must be. Then our bathtubs fill and we drift in the water, with gentle ripples and splashes, until the drain clanks and I move quickly, so that our two nude bodies land on the tile floor together.

Now there is a silent empty time before we will become even closer. The kitchens are on opposite sides of our studio apartments. I drink orange juice and coffee alone. Then I return to the bathroom and wait for the sudden metallic thud of the medicine cabinet door. We are facing each other, brushing our teeth. And then I can hear, or almost hear, a small creaking sound as she seats herself.

Soon the morning is over for me. Her door bangs shut, muffled steps pass by. I go back to bed. I usually linger there, dozing and reading magazines, until it's time for lunch and the soap operas. Unless the phone rings: my children trying to get me to go out. When I've refused for months, they threaten to visit, forcing me to agree to meet at a coffee shop rather than have my home invaded. And, of course, they will report back to that impossible woman, their mother.

Normally I remain home. If I do go out, I have to be careful to get back before six, when she usually returns. I can't take the risk of being caught in the corridor, having to turn my back and bend my body while I frantically unlock my door and disappear inside. She mustn't see how old I am, and I mustn't see how old she may be. My few accidental and averted glimpses of her at her doorway have been of well-rounded shoulders and back, nothing inconsistent with the voluptuous body in the bathtub.

Evenings are not always easy. The tremor of her TV usually isn't loud enough for me to be sure I'm with her. Popular shows like *Dallas* and *Dynasty* are no problem. But sometimes music, applause, or laughter from her apartment suddenly makes me realize we are not watching together. Then I keep turning the dial, hoping to find where she is.

After eleven, nothing intrudes on us. Most nights we casually move into sleep, as I dream myself into her dreams. Often I stroll the Left Bank with her, or we embrace in a dark corner of a nightclub in New York. Soon we're asleep together. But sometimes her bed bumps against the wall and startles me, changing the course of my night. I like to think it's an unconscious sign of her desire; or even better, that it's deliberate. When I hear or imagine it, or some other sound, a stirring or a sigh, I feel challenged. Then I will enter her warm flesh. The effort—my hand between my legs, moving slowly and for a long time, in order to satisfy her—leaves me exhausted; while she sleeps silently in the next room. **Q**

Let me be clear. When I say that I want *The New York Times* to make changes, I do not mean that I want it to make change. That would be thoughtful, but the people at the Manhattanite, the deli around the corner, handle that for me. Furthermore, I will not take issue at the present time with the shocking quality of the *Times*'s newsprint. The ashen smear left after even the most cursory survey of the paper is vexing, but it does have its perks for Western security: KGB agents who have read the Real Estate section of the Sunday *Times* can be traced by the CIA for seven days.

Of more substantial concern are the lapses in style so frequent that they should not be called "lapses" at all. I only used the word "lapses" because I have lent my thesaurus to an actress down the hall who is writing reviews about herself for some postcards she is sending around and I couldn't think of another word. For instance, why must the *Times* divide its stories the way it does? I can't count how often in a day I begin a story in the "A" section only to learn that it is continued in the "D" section, miles from there. I am thus forced to hunt back and forth between column bottoms and column tops: first I must flip forward to find the continuation of the story, and then I must flip backward to find the original story, having forgotten what the last word of the first part was, and then I must hurriedly flip back forward to find the first word of the last part before forgetting again what the last word of the first part was. What perverted puritan ethic asks a paying reader to work like this? It is the reporter's job to find the news, not the reader's.

Only a single circumstance could justify this jarring editorial practice. If President Reagan was in the Rose Garden and told reporters, "In my mind, no one I can think of in my administration has committed what I view to be a crimi—" and then sprinted into Lincoln's Bedroom and made them find him before concluding, "—nal act," then it would be one thing for the *Times* to break it that way. But President Reagan is unlikely to do such a thing, especially after all his surgery. If a busy man like the President can complete his thoughts in one place, so can the *Times*.

Another puzzling mark of the paper is the special treatment it accords certain reporters. This favoritism manifests itself in the small phrase "Special to *The New York Times*," which appears, in finer type, under select authors' bylines. I first spotted it under Hedrick Smith's byline. At the time, I thought it awfully sweet. Hedrick Smith was special to me, too: he had gone to Choate, where I had gone, and had spoken at my graduation. Why his speaking at my graduation, which, after all, was eleven years ago, should make him special to *The New York Times* I could not say, but I was flattered nevertheless.

Mr. Smith was not the only correspondent so recognized: William Schmidt, Stephen Engleberg, John Noble Wilford— surely they could not all have spoken at Choate without my knowing it. It seemed that everyone was special to the *Times*. But then, one day, I saw that some correspondents were more special than others. On that day, the front page sported stories by eight correspondents. Seven were special to *The New York Times* and one was not: poor Maureen Dowd! Maureen Dowd, who had labored long and hard over her story, going without meals sometimes, and finally, as she raced toward press time, missing the first act of *Big River*, a musical she had wanted to see since it opened, because once, for a whole summer when she was a little girl, she had dreamed of making a musical of *Huckleberry Finn*. (I'm guessing about all this—I don't know Miss Dowd.) How do the editors think this little snub made her feel? Things are hard enough for her already, being named Dowd. The *Times* would do well to remember the words of my preschool teacher Mrs. Giblin: "He who calls his friend special is as he who brings water to the thirsting flower: both will blossom and bear beauty." Actually, I'm sorry, I was confused. Kahlil Gibran said that. Mrs. Giblin said, "Spill that finger paint again and you can clean it up with your tongue!"

Most articles in the paper are signed, except the editorials, which is standard newspaper policy across the nation, and the television listings, the national policy of which I do not know. It is the television page that is home to the paper's most rankling offenses.

For example, when a movie is scheduled to appear on television, the film's title is listed, followed by the year of the movie's release, a couple of its cast members, and a brief remark from an unnamed critic. In theory I like this. With all there is for a man to do these days—not only must we hold a job and do exercises, but we are expected to take an interest in home furnishings as well—I am just as happy to let the *Times* recommend a movie. However, frequently I run up against this:

A Pompom for the President (1941) Deanna Durbin, Don Ameche, Patsy Kelly. Not reviewed by us.

For a reviewer to write as his review, "Not reviewed by us," requires a certain nerve. If I had been glancing through the stock quotations and between Polaroid and Poptals had seen *Pompom for Prez—Nt Rvwd by Us,* that I could accept. It is not the responsibility of the *Times*'s financial analysts to review *A Pompom for the President,* however much the President's receiving or not receiving that pompom might affect his handling of the economy.

If this negligent practice is to continue, the reviewer might at least offer a proper excuse:

Skating and Dying (1979) Swiss drama. Not reviewed by us. Had to take Billy to the orthodontist.

The *Times* also includes, against my every wish, cable listings on the television page. I can't afford cable and I hate to be reminded of it by seeing what the people who can afford it are getting—it is the height of mean-spiritedness. By the same logic, the paper should send out cards that read, "Champagne brunch with delicious free food and lots of people who will help you get a job. Invitation only. This is not an invitation."

If the *Times* insists on printing these listings, it should be mature and print them in a secret ink that only cable subscribers could read. Failing that, it should display a little sympathy. For example:

> *Casablanca* (1942) Humphrey Bogart, Ingrid Bergman. Unintelligible claptrap about WWII in Morocco. Everyone knows all good WWII stuff is in England or France. Here's not looking at you.

I have confined the bulk of this discussion to the front and back pages of the paper. I have not discussed the inside pages because I do not read them. I am proud to say I have rarely read the "B" section, and now that they've moved the Quote of the Day out of it, I never do so.

To be honest, I am afraid to open the paper. First, I never learned that folding trick that everyone else seems to know, and second, I can't forget what happened to Aunt Kit. My great-aunt Kit was reading the paper on one of the new benches just outside the Children's Zoo in Central Park. She opened the paper to finish an article that was continued inside. As she did, the breeze surged and she was smothered, ironically by the Living Section.

We were sad, of course, but, being churchgoers, were fortified to know that, like the article which killed her, Aunt Kit is continued in another place. **Q**

Here is what I will do when I turn over my new leaf:
I will eat right. I'll be healthy.
I will ask Meredith to marry me.
I will learn how to sleep. I will sleep long and well.
I will be prompt, competent, and cheerful at my place of employment. With my co-workers I will exchange pleasant, clever trivialities.
Really, I mean it—I will. I'll try.

Here is what I will not do when I turn over my new leaf:
I will not stop to examine crumbling slips of paper that I find on the street.
I will not place late-night, long-distance phone calls to obscure former friends in a falsely hearty tone.
Ditto rambling letters. Control, control.
I will not neglect Meredith weeks at a time.
Neither will I pray. No crutches, motherfucker.

Here is what I etc.—
Meet a woman named Meredith.
Take her to a quiet place and explain about my pain. **Q**

My mother told me the wondrous news as I was dressing for school that morning. My father was taking the afternoon off from work to take me to see a movie; just the two of
us, like on a date. And my father would bring my lunch with
him when he came, my mother said. And she said not to
breathe a word of it to anyone, not even to my teacher, especially not to my teacher. My father would come and, if my
teacher didn't like it, tough, my mother said, and then my
mother laughed the way she laughed when it was just between
us girls.

I boarded the school bus in a daze. It was the first time my
father was going to do something just with me, and the wonder
of it gripped me, and I felt like one of those animated cartoon
characters who gets clobbered over the head and sees stars
and hears birds chirping as he staggers like a drunk to regain
his balance. And I was afraid, and I hated myself for being
afraid, and that only made it worse.

All that morning, I kept sneaking a peek at the square pane
of glass in our classroom door, a window that often revealed
the principal's face as he peered in, smiled, nodded. In an
hour, in half an hour, any minute now, that window would
reveal my father's face; and I kept wishing my mother hadn't
talked him into taking an afternoon off from work to fetch me
to see a movie; just the two of us, as if on a date. And I prayed
I would be good, that I wouldn't do or say anything that would
upset my father and make him wish he were somewhere else,
with someone else. All that morning, I sat at my desk and I
wished and I prayed. I was ten years old and in the fifth grade.

I heard his knock, polite but persistent, and I saw his
face showing in the small window in our classroom door. I

watched as Mrs. Chapman pushed herself up from behind her desk and, with a quizzical look, went to open the door. And I heard my father say, in a voice that said, What I am telling you is a fact, not a request, "I've come to get my daughter."

I saw Mrs. Chapman look over at me and then back to my father, and then she spoke to him in a soft voice I couldn't hear, and as she spoke in the soft voice I couldn't hear, she moved between the half-open door and the doorjamb, blocking my father's way into the room, or maybe trying to block out my catching sight of him. But he was a tall man, my father was, and I could see the polite but determined look on his face, and I heard him say, in the same voice he had used before, "I'll take complete responsibility."

Then I saw my father look over Mrs. Chapman's head to me, and he said, "Sunny, let's go," and made a let's-go motion with his arm, a gesture that looked to me as if it had more determination than it had comfort in it.

I saw the teacher move aside and watch me as I came out from behind my desk. I could see all of my father now, and in his other hand, which hung sort of laxly at his side, I saw a small brown bag. I walked past Mrs. Chapman, through the open door, and on out into the wide hall; and my father and I walked down the wide, silent hall, without speaking and without holding hands. At the school door, my father pushed in the bar that released the lock and pushed open the door. He used only one hand to do it, and that impressed me. I needed both my hands to open the door, and all my weight behind them, too.

My father went out into the warm spring day first, and I, walking on his shadow as if it were a carpet that had been thrown down for my feet, followed him down the steps. I saw our car parked right in front of the school for all the world to see, brazen, just as my father had been at the door of my classroom. All the windows were rolled down, and once I had settled in the passenger seat and my father behind the wheel, my father dropped the paper bag in my lap and said, "You had better eat this now. I'll buy you a Coke when we get there."

I took out an American cheese sandwich on Wonder bread spread with mayonnaise, the top slice lumpy with pieces of sour pickle, and began to eat. The sandwich was hard to swallow without something to wash it down with, and in my eagerness to be done with it, the bites I took were too big. My father warned me to slow down, not to take such big bites, and I felt ugly with my mouth full, and I wanted to spit out what I had in my mouth. I kept on eating, with my mouth carefully closed. I even smoothed and folded the bag the way I had been taught to do when I was finished.

We had to circle the block a few times before my father found an empty parking space. I stood back behind him when he purchased our tickets. I said, "Yes, sir," when he asked me if I wanted a Coke and "No, sir," when he asked me if I wanted popcorn to go along with the Coke. When I said, "No, sir," to the popcorn, I saw my father frown. Now I wish that he had asked me again so that I could have said, "Yes, sir," and pleased him.

The movie was called *The Best Years of Our Lives* and it was about three war veterans. During the ride home, my father tried to strike up a conversation with me about the movie we had just seen. Had I enjoyed it? What did I think about this fellow or that fellow? Did I think they would live happily ever after? But all he got for his troubles was a lot of I-don't-knows and What-do-you-thinks?—childishnesses that I could see were getting on my father's nerves and, oh, how I prayed to be home in a hurry.

When we turned into our driveway, my mother came rushing out to the porch: all smiles, one playful clap of her hands as she hurried down the porch steps to greet us. Had we had a good time? Wasn't I proud of my father for taking the afternoon off to be with me for a movie? Didn't I know now how much my father loved me, even though he didn't always let it show the way other fathers maybe did?

And soon my mother was serving us our supper, in silence, as she usually did.

We ate it in silence, as we usually did.

And that silence comforted me, as it always did, and left me free to wonder why my father had come into the school with my sandwich with him instead of leaving it in the car until I was settled in the seat and he was behind the wheel, and to wonder why I had felt so ashamed of myself for taking such big bites; free to wonder and to feel ashamed, and to wish I had said "Yes, sir" when my father had offered me the popcorn to go along with the Coke. **Q**

My father, with his jeweler's eye, saw it coming and burned his Party card with a gas jet used to solder gold. He said, Today I am a Peronista. Today you are a Peronista's daughter. But what my father did not see was that the soldier who circled our house looking for him found me. He said, Your father is a Communist. And you are a Communist's daughter.

My father said that he was a Communist not for the Party doctrine but for the Party doctors and dentists. The Communists had free medicine. My father had bad teeth. My father cast his own extracted teeth in gold and would have set them in his mouth himself, but here his craft fell short and he was forced to rely on the clumsy expertise of the dentists.

Would a Communist have a mouthful of gold? my father asked the police, opening wide. But the police were unimpressed and the soldier continued his patrol.

From the soldier's car, parked on the Calle Anchorena, I could hear Libertad Lamarque taking her singing lesson. I mouthed the words as she sang them, one hand on my heart and one hand extended, opening wide for the high notes. Together we did "Besos Brujos"; we did "Tomo y Obligo"; we did "Mano a Mano." When we finished "Mano a Mano," the soldier applauded, and when he finished applauding, he closed his fingers around the wrist of my extended arm. He said, Put your hand here.

I said, I know where to put my hand.

My father said that if he had had a machine that could do what his hands could do, he would have been a rich man—and I would have been a rich man's daughter. Before my father became a jeweler, his first job was painting wood grain on steel bed frames. Compared to trompe l'oeil, my father said, making passports is easy. But making money is still hard.

When my father found out the price I was paying for his protection, he clenched his gilded teeth and said nothing.

He said nothing until he said that I was as good as gold, that I had a heart of gold, that I was worth my weight in gold. I was precious metal in my father's eyes. He said he knew I would not turn on him.

The soldier said, If you do not do as I say, I will turn your father in. I said, If you turn my father in, I will not do as you say. I had him, as they say, in the palm of my hand. And no machine could do what my hands could do.

The soldier's car came to be as well known on the Calle Anchorena as the well-attended singing lessons of Libertad Lamarque. While she crooned her tangos, I worked the buttons of the soldier's woolen uniform. Afterward, we would sit unmoving in the car's front seat and listen to a final ballad, Libertad Lamarque's voice breaking over the notes while the soldier hummed softly, eyes closed, palms turned up in his lap.

Sometime later, Libertad Lamarque called Evita a whore and left for Mexico on the same night. At least she did not have to give up her language, my father said.

My father cast lead in the form of the national insignia. He carved pieces of inner tube into the words ASIV TIX3. He bound small books in blue leather and refined the signature of the Argentine consul. But my father did not make Libertad Lamarque's passport. He would have if she'd asked him. He would have made hers for free. He would have made mine, too —but I would not sit for the photograph.

When the soldier asked my father for his daughter's hand, my father did not see it coming. **Q**

I've lived near a city all my life, except for three years at law school—and a few summers, when I was a kid, at a golf camp in the Poconos. Those times didn't matter much, though; I always knew I could go home again. I spent most of my winters in city schools and at the university; most of my summers I spent hanging around swimming pools at local country clubs. Once I knew how to sign my name, I knew I'd never go hungry.

My wife and I live these days in the country. "It's *country,*" we like to tell our old friends on the phone. We like to say, "It is *good* here," too. Sometimes I'm afraid these may be the final words on what's become of us; but we live only two hours from downtown Pittsburgh—about ninety miles north of the city, where the land begins rippling Midwestern monotony into the foothills of the Alleghenies—and it really is quite pleasant here. We live in the backyard of a farmer whose name is Ed, in a drafty old farmhouse Ed's great-grandfather built a long time ago for his bride. In our own backyard, there's a natural pond Ed keeps nicely stocked with fish; in the summer months, we often see him passing by our kitchen window with a fishing pole and a net. Beyond the pond, but before the woods that cover the land until, in the far distance, the property of the Jackson County Sewage Treatment Plant begins, there is a cornfield; in the fall, early in the evenings, I watch Ed heading that way with a shotgun and his dog. Sometimes he stops at our back door, bearing the bounty of his land: smallmouth bass in the summer; then later, during the harvest, the birds —plucked and gutted, oddly unrelated to the brilliantly colored limp things he and the dog carry home from the cornfield after hunting.

When the birds are legally in season, Ed occasionally invites me to accompany him and his dog on their hunts. I take these invitations as compliments: there aren't many country clubs around here, and the worst thing I ever heard Ed say about another man was "I'd rather not spend the whole day in a duck blind with him."

"Come on, son," he likes to say to me. "Let's try some hunting."

He likes to say, too, "We'll leave the women at home."

"What the hell, Ed," I always say.

It's like this: Margot and I have been married just under a year. We still like doing things just with each other. We like working around each other during the day in town; after hours, we like settling down together in the house Ed's great-grandfather built. Sometimes we sit together with work we've brought home from our offices; more often, we relax with a bottle of something or other and one of our favorite television shows. When we were *just* married, a business associate of our families, whose name we have both forgotten, gave us a television set for a wedding present. At first, we kept the thing locked in the root cellar, sealed in its original, moisture-proof, "Just-Married!" gift wrapping. After a while, we began using it as a soothing climax to the long days. We even moved the thing upstairs to a bedroom closet. Now we set it up almost every night. We hold hands in bed, watching our favorite shows.

"Sweetheart," Margot likes to say at such hours of the night, "I want you to have a good time with your friends."

And I always answer, "But Ed's not my friend."

A funny thing about all this is that, also inside the bedroom closet—behind, as a matter of fact, the television set —there are three shotguns. We keep them buried underneath a dirty laundry bag, which is monogrammed with our new conjugal initials (it was another wedding present). The guns lie there in long black-leather attaché cases, a bit like business reports ready for the next board of directors meeting. They

ROB PRICE

were my grandfather's guns; he gave them to me on my
twenty-first birthday. "You should learn how to use these,
Robbie," he said to me on that occasion. "You've always been
such a silly kid." There are two 12-gauge shotguns in the
collection, and one 20-gauge I think my grandfather used on
doves. One of the 12's is a side-by-side; the other is an over-
and-under. The over-and-under is engraved with silver and
gold and was given to my grandfather by a South American
dictator whose name I have never been able to remember. The
gun was custom-built according to my grandfather's height
(just about mine) and weight (mine exactly) and strength (I
think his was the greater). Each of the guns rests disassembled
in its own case, and comes with two or three barrel assemblies
of varying lengths and diameters, the choice of which, I am
told, depends largely upon what you intend to shoot at on any
particular occasion. Actually, Ed is the one who told me this.
Ed also likes showing me how to put the guns together and
take them apart. There may be something funny about this,
too, for since my grandfather now is a very old man, he cannot
remember how, and I have never been able to figure the damn
things out.

Before the shotguns, the only firearm I owned was a .22
rifle. My father gave it to me on my sixth birthday. It was a
good gun for a boy: it was a single-shot, bolt-action weapon,
fitted with a peep sight instead of the more exotic telescopic
device, and after my birthday party, my father and I drove to
a nearby stone quarry to shoot at old tin cans and birthday
balloons. It was a good day; it was a *sporting* day. The following
summer, my grandfather gathered himself and his own sons
on the company plane and they all flew together to Africa for
some real sport on the plains of Kenya. There were no tin cans
on that trip; there were lions and leopards, Cape buffalo and
elephants, and so many varieties of the antelope family that,
as my grandfather grew older, he could never distinguish the
stuffed remains of one from another. He would say to friends,
"That's an impala," when actually the thing he was pointing

at had once been the head of an eland, or a Thomson's gazelle, or even a kongoni; it didn't matter, really: nobody else knew the differences between the animals, either. But the remains of their many individual lives occupied the walls and floors and coffee tables of what our family used to call the Head House, and my cousins and I used to enjoy the company of these things in a weird kind of way whenever we got high there or drank my grandfather's liquor. We were just a hundred yards from the main house; we could always hear the adults entertaining themselves up there in their own fashion, and where we were, there were wild animal hooves inlaid with sterling-silver ashtrays for our own deposits, and on the walls were stuffed heads and hanging skins and ivory tusks that we liked to run our hands over when it was late and we were good and stoned. And there was also a book, bound in the skin of a lion, that we liked to thumb through at such times, for it contained copies of all the licenses my grandfather had purchased in order to shoot each animal: one license per head, to make the killing legal.

Why do I keep these guns? It is difficult to explain (and I suspect my explanations). My reasons change from day to day; I can't remember how they all got started. Our insurance man assures me the guns are collector's pieces; he thinks I should convert them into a down payment on a house or a trust fund to properly educate the children Margot and I must intend to have. We could get on with our lives, he tells me. "Your premiums would be cheaper," he says.

"What the hell, Tom," I always answer, though Margot assures me the man's name is Frank.

It's like this (I think): every now and then—if Margot's not at home—I enjoy swinging one of the side-by-sides around the house. I'll be in the bedroom usually—just gunning down the odd hallucination that flies through the open window from time to time. "Swing through," I'll tell myself. And: "*Snap* that trigger." Once a month, I even oil and polish the old things. When they are clean, I enjoy resting the stock of each piece on the floor and peering into the barrels. There's nothing much to see, but out of the darkness comes the sweet smell of Hoppe's No. 9 Nitro Powder Solvent, and memories: the soft kick of a .22; old tin cans; birthday balloons.

I remember the Head House smelling pleasant in the summer, like a well-cleaned stable, and in the winter months, the glass eyes of the animal heads glittered in the dark and we fell asleep in front of the fireplace on zebra-skin rugs. By day, the eyes became marbles again, and all the animals had the same blank expression. The cats were an exception: their faces were frozen in a timeless snarl. And there was one leopard who had no head at all: his neck ended abruptly, sprouting at its tip two incongruous spotted ears.

We moved here after we got married. Margot had landed a job in the local offices of the State Department of Environmental Resources. I joined a small law firm in town about a month later. We often do work for local government authorities; one of our best-paying clients these days is the Jackson County Sewage and Water Authority, whose sewage-treatment plant Margot and I can smell in our backyard when the wind is just right. It is a sour, innardly sort of smell, and it comes from the direction of Ed's cornfield.

For everything (says Ed) there is a season. In the fall, I enjoy watching Ed plucking up his own harvests. Wild game birds spring into the air in front of his tractor; they fly or run like hell toward the nearest hedgerow or copse of trees. Early that evening, I'll hear the distant boom of Ed's shotgun: one shot usually; sometimes a double, if the earth is feeling generous.

One day, when Margot was out of town, Ed put the shotguns together for me and we carried them outside. After a while, we laid the shotguns in a patch of grass and stood over them. They looked attractive there; I imagined some dead birds draped beside them. I imagined a photograph of something my family has only a thousand other shots of.

"I read about your grandfather's stroke," Ed said all of a sudden. "It was in the papers."

"I know," I said. "We tried to hush it up."

"No kidding," said Ed. "How do you do that?"

"I'm not sure," I said. "It didn't work."

The day was dropping away from us. I watched the sun easing toward a low line of pine trees somewhere near Ohio. Margot was in Pittsburgh, shopping or some such thing. I was supposed to be planting bulbs for next spring.

"I have some number-six shells in the house," I said. "In both gauges."

Ed looked at his watch. He said, "Okay. I'll get the dog."

Upstairs in our bedroom, I found an old corduroy hunting shirt someone had given me. The shirt had a big pocket stitched across the back. I found the shotgun shells, too, hidden in my sock drawer. I stuffed them into the pockets of the hunting shirt. The shirt felt pleasant with the pockets full. They had never been full before.

Outside, Ed was waiting with the dog. A silver bell dangled from the dog's collar. When he saw Ed and me pick up the guns, the dog jumped up and the bell rang.

"Find a bird, Mike," Ed said.

Mike took off toward the pond. A bunch of starlings hit the air as he charged through them. They made the sky turn dark. Mike didn't even glance at them. He was headed for the cornfield.

Ed and I ran after him. We held the shotguns across our chests with both hands. Ed had my grandfather's 20-gauge and I was carrying the 12. Ed said it was probably too much gun for pheasant; I said that was all right, I wasn't too much of a hunter. It felt funny running with the gun; I kept rubbing the safety with my thumb. We ran through the backyard, past some forsythia Margot and I had planted, then down the slope through tall, sharp grass toward the pond.

Mike was there already, wagging his tail and sniffing around a bed of honeysuckle. "Find a bird, Mike," Ed said. Ed held his gun the way I had seen my grandfather holding his in old photographs. The muzzle was pointed at the ground, and the weight of the gun was supported on his bent forearm, with the end of the stock stuck in his armpit. I kept shifting the 12-gauge from arm to arm. It was heavy as hell. It got heavier, too, as Ed and I walked around the pond and turned into the cornfield.

The cornfield was full of brown stubble. Ears of dead corn lay in between the rows of stubble. The ears were turning dark; they looked like the stuff Margot likes to hang on the front door during the fall. "Listen," said Ed, but I couldn't hear anything.

"His bell's stopped ringing," Ed said. Then his gun was in both arms and he was running across the field and toward the woods on the other side. I grabbed my gun just like that and started running after him. We ran over a rise and saw the dog standing alongside a low hedge of brambles. "Find the bird, Mike," Ed said, and followed the dog. I followed Ed.

"What am I supposed to be looking for?" I said.

"Watch the dog," Ed said.

The thing about all this is that, about a week later, my grandfather sent me a Masai spear for my birthday. It's a long, serious-looking spear, with one blunt end you stick in the ground, and the other end you catch the leaping body of a lion upon, if a lion happens to be leaping upon you, I suppose. I called my grandfather to thank him. His secretary told me she'd thought I would like it. Then she connected me with my grandfather.

"Hello?" he said.

"Hello, Grampa," I said. "It's Rob."

"Rob who?" he said.

"It's me, Robbie, Grampa," I said.

"Oh, hello, Robbie," he said.

"I shot a bird last week," I told him.

"Really?" he said. "What kind of bird?"

"It was a beautiful bird, Grampa," I said.

We were quiet with each other then—an awkward way to be on the phone.

Finally I said, "Margot cooked it. It was very good."

"Good," he said. "Who's Margot?"

"My wife," I said.

"Oh," he said.

"Are you okay, Grampa?" I said.

"I'm okay," he said. "It's just that I've forgotten whom I'm talking to."

"Rob," I said. "It's me, Robbie."

"Oh, hello, Robbie," my grandfather said.

Last week, Margot filed suit on behalf of the DER, accusing the Sewage and Water Authority of dumping raw sewage into French Creek. The county wants to take the suit to court; the commissioners think a courtroom brawl will be cheaper than building a new sewage-treatment plant. They are wrong in this opinion. They do not know that after the dust has settled, they will still have to build a new plant and pay their attorneys' fees.

Just one more funny thing about all this is that I am the attorney assigned to the county's defense. At the first meeting with our clients, I remarked that our sewage-disposal problems struck me as a perfect metaphor for the human condition. Nobody cracked a smile. I got serious then and said I expected this fight to last about five years. Everyone smiled. It was the beginning of a long and beautiful friendship.

Margot and I spend a lot of our time nowadays studying the legal history of municipal sewage disposal. At night we try to relax within whispering distance of each other. We hold hands, watch TV, and wonder from week to week how *L.A. Law* will leave its various conflicts unresolved. We also wonder how Harry Hamlin and Susan Dey will manage to balance their public responsibilities against their private needs. We know they have a conflict of interest.

I suppose that's all I want to say. Certainly I have no interest in the particulars of this fellow Ed's life. I have no interest in knowing where his money comes from, or whether he farms for a profit. I have no idea whether he stocks his land with birds raised in coops, or what his wife and he talk about in bed. What I want, I think, more than I want most other things, is to keep this man free of these entanglements.

I think I have, you see, my uses for him. **Q**

Sorry, sorry, been underground. And been out sick the last week or so, so missed your call. Now I'm back, but leaving for the dreaded ABA and today is my day to get organized for it. Thank you for keeping track of me—I've been getting used to a new situation these past few months and so haven't surfaced very often, but here I am. The new situation is that the person I more or less live with has AIDS, and I've been getting used to that—as much as I can. It's odd how the most real crisis in some weird way becomes the most clichéd. We've had to get through the "No, I'm not going to desert you because you're ill" period and then settle into whatever this new life will be. Don't have a fuck of an idea what it will be, because there is lots of pretense on his part that this isn't happening. I'm willing to play along for the moment and am trying to suppress my usual relentlessness about forcing every issue so that it becomes clear. It is hard to tell, though, when one is simply generating bad karma by wanting to discuss every inevitability. I don't want to corrupt an essentially optimistic person with my morbidity. For the moment, we can pretend that nothing is too much amiss, since he feels generally well. AZT is an amazing substance for a while—until it becomes a poison and reacts against the body. But that usually isn't for a year or so. A friend of mine is dying at the moment after a miraculous year on AZT. It is disconcerting to speak, on the one hand, to someone who is convinced the drug is saving him while, on the other hand, someone else is telling you how it has destroyed his bone marrow and liver. But it is possible to do, I guess. There's always the chance that someone will have a different response. I don't believe it, though. Sometimes I feel as if I am living in a television movie-of-the-week with all the usual melodrama. Am spending all my money on planning vacations and things: small, pointless tricks like: if I pay for the most expensive opera subscription through next March, then he can't die until then, because the tickets are paid for. Once the opera season is over, I'm not sure what I'll come up with. But something. As for myself, I feel great and think I have never looked better. There is something about taking care of someone else that turns the attention away from one's own body. Perhaps one tends to thrive almost perversely. And so am thriving—as well as being very happy at work. In a certain sense, things have never been better. We're going to go away after the ABA—my friend has always wanted to go to Disneyland. I'm flying him to meet me there. See what I mean about a TV movie? It's like one of those children in the *National Enquirer* who have that aging disease—they always want to go to Disneyland. There's not much I'd rather not do more than spend the day in an amusement park with fat women in pantsuits and their children. But I will ride the Mad Hatter's Teacups, or whatever you do there, and like it. As a child, I never went on a ride, even a merry-go-round, without vomiting. Hope my stomach has matured, even if my brain hasn't. I'll scrawl again soon. But every day you are in my heart, and always with love. **Q**

She was afraid
he was going to
get violent
again

© 89